Talk About
ENGLISH

How Words Travel and Change

BY **JANET KLAUSNER**

ILLUSTRATIONS BY NANCY DONIGER

Thomas Y. Crowell   New York

Library of Congress Cataloging-in-Publication Data
Klausner, Janet.
  Talk about English : how words travel and change / by Janet
Klausner; illustrations by Nancy Doniger.
      p.   cm.
  Includes bibliographical references.
  Summary: Traces the development of the English language from its
earliest beginnings to modern English, explaining how individual words
evolved as a result of events in English history, and through usage.
  ISBN 0-690-04831-9. —ISBN 0-690-04833-5 (lib. bdg.)
  1. English language—Etymology—Juvenile literature.   2. English
language—History—Juvenile literature.   [1. English language—
Etymology.   2. English language—History.]   I. Doniger, Nancy,
ill.   II. Title.
PE1574.K48   1990   89-49116
422—dc20   CIP
                                                       AC

Grateful acknowledgment is made to the following for permission to reprint the
materials below:

Her Majesty's Stationery Office, for an excerpt from a speech by Winston
Churchill to the House of Commons, June 4, 1940, *Hansard*, columns 787–96.
Reprinted by permission of Her Majesty's Stationery Office, Norwich, England.

Harcourt Brace Jovanovich, Inc., for use of "Buffalo Dusk" from *Smoke and
Steel* by Carl Sandburg, copyright 1920 by Harcourt Brace Jovanovich, Inc. and
renewed 1948 by Carl Sandburg, reprinted by permission of the publisher.

Little, Brown and Company, for use of "My Dream" from *Verses from 1929 On*
by Ogden Nash, copyright 1954 by Ogden Nash. Copyright © renewed 1982 by
Frances Nash, Isabel Nash Eberstadt and Linnell Nash Smith. First appeared in *The
New Yorker.* By permission of Little, Brown and Company.

ACKNOWLEDGMENTS

Grateful acknowledgment is offered to Elizabeth Baer for her expertise in linguistics, her thoughtful reading, and her helpful advice. The author also wishes to express gratitude to these friends and colleagues, among the most astute of all editors of writing for young readers, for their careful readings and encouragement: Joanne Fedorocko, Wendy Gaal, Tanner Ottley Gay, and Barbara Hainley.

Contents

Talk About ENGLISH

Introduction

Try to imagine yourself in each of these scenes.

Scene 1. You are hungry. In your hand is a deep-red, shiny apple. You take a bite. It tastes fresh and cool and juicy, doesn't it? "MMMMMMMMM," you say.

Look at the apple. Oh, no! A fat worm is wiggling inside it! Now you sputter something else: "YECCH!" or "UGH!" or even "PTUI!"

Scene 2. A close friend is talking to you. You nod now and then to show that you're listening. Once in a while, you make low agreeing sounds, like these: "Hmmmmm . . . uh-hmmmm . . . uh-hmmmm."

Your friend says something funny. "Ha ha ha ha ha ha," you laugh, with short barking noises.

Your friend continues, mentioning something that is sad. You shake your head to show that you feel pity. Placing your tongue against the upper back of your front teeth, you make quick little sympathetic noises, something like *ts ts ts ts ts ts.*

1

Scene 3. You are standing in a crowded bus. An unusually large person steps hard on your foot. What do you say? "OWWWWWW"? "OOOOOOOOOH"? How about "YAAAAAAAAAAAAAAAH"?

In these three scenes, you expressed your delight, your disgust, your distress—you communicated your feelings. And you did it in a way that felt perfectly natural. You used your lips and tongue and teeth and voice to make noises.

We are accustomed to such noises. The gentle coo that lulls a baby to sleep, the *shhh* that leads to silence, the smacking sound of a kiss—all have meaning. Yells, sighs, clicks, grunts, snorts, whistles, and hums are familiar sounds to us. All help us to communicate.

Of course, human beings are not the only living things that communicate with mouth-and-voice noises. Squeals and squeaks and howls and growls abound in the animal kingdom. When animals make those sounds, they are communicating messages, too. But there is a difference. An important one.

Sometime in the long-distant past, our prehistoric ancestors began to use sounds in new ways, distinctly human ways. The shape of their vocal tract was changing, so they could make more kinds of sounds. And their brains were larger, so they could think about the meanings of things. They could make connections between sound and meaning. They could create *words.* Only in human language do words name things, feelings, and ideas. When the words are put together, they describe how those things, feelings, and ideas are related. It is the special human ability to connect words with meaning that enables you to describe not only what you are doing right now ("I'm reading") but also what you were doing four hours ago, and what you plan to be doing twenty-four hours from now (and millions of other wonderfully complicated messages like those).

We will probably never know how or when words were first used to communicate. But we do know that to be a word user is to be a human being. The first word users may have been the first human beings.

Over many thousands of years, those earliest human beings learned to be hunters, farmers, toolmakers, builders, and artists. They also became expert word makers.

Our curiosity about our prehistoric ancestors has led us to find out many things about their tools, art, buildings, and way of life. We are also learning how those early people used words.

Say this word: *star.* Listen to its sounds: *star.* Think about its meaning. Perhaps you picture a twinkling point of light in a black sky. Perhaps, if you have an interest in science, you picture a broiling mass of gas like our sun. You might picture a gold sticker on a perfect spelling test. Or an actor taking a bow. The word *star* makes us think of many things. Where did it get its sounds and its meanings?

Is it possible that someone in an ancient time, gazing at a night sky, suddenly snapped two fingers and announced, "I know! Let's call them *stars*"?

No, it's not possible. It is true that words sometimes seem to come into the English language suddenly. But they almost never arrive fully formed, as if dropped out of the blue.

A word is a traveler. Because its journey is long, and because it makes many stops, its exact starting point may be unclear. As a word travels and is shared among different groups of people, it changes. It may grow longer or shorter. The sounds within it are uttered in different ways by different speakers.

For the past two hundred years, scholars have made remarkable progress in tracing the roots of the languages that are spoken today. Language explorers face tasks that are time-consuming and difficult. But the hard work is worth it, if the reward is the fascinating rediscovery of the past.

Anyone who wants to learn about the past must look for clues. A small piece of a buried bowl may be a clue to a prehistoric village. A fossilized footprint may be a clue to a long-extinct dinosaur. Explorers of prehistoric languages, however, cannot dig up clues from the ground. Their search is for languages that no one ever wrote down, languages that no one has heard for thousands of years. Their job might seem impossible, but language explorers know where to look for traces of those early languages. They know that clues are all around us. The clues are hidden in the words we speak today.

Language scholars compare many languages, those still spoken today along with ancient ones for which there are written records. By comparing the words in all those languages, they find similar patterns of sounds. Here, for example, are words from four modern languages and two ancient ones (Latin originated in ancient Rome, Sanskrit in ancient India).

English	German	French	Spanish	Latin	Sanskrit
mother	Mutter	mère	madre	mater	matar-
night	Nacht	nuit	noche	nox	nakta
sun	Sonne	soleil	sol	sol	surya
three	drei	trois	tres	tres	trayas

Examining the patterns in such words helps scholars reconstruct lost-but-not-forgotten languages of the past. In that painstaking way, language scholars have pieced together one prehistoric language that is the root of many modern languages, including English.

About six thousand years ago, that prehistoric language was shared by people living somewhere in northern Europe or western Asia—no one knows exactly where. In that language was a word that probably sounded like *ster.* Time passed, and the word traveled and changed. It changed not just into our modern English word *star,* but also into space-related terms such as *constellation, asteroid, astronomy,* and *astronaut;* into the flower name *aster* (the rays of an aster are like the points of a star); into the word *disaster* (bad luck used to be attributed to the stars); and into names like *Esther* and *Stella.*

Scholars called that parent language Proto-Indo-European (*Proto* from a Greek word that means "first"; and *Indo-European* from the geographical area that was the early home of daughter languages).

Over thousands of years, the parent language took different routes among different peoples. Its descendants include languages that are now as different as the Polish of Poland and the Hindi of India. The version of English that we speak today is only several hundred years old. But its roots go back to the same Proto-Indo-European ancestor of numerous modern and ancient languages.

Because the English language is always moving, always changing, it gathers new words all the time. Some of those new words appear abruptly, as if out of nowhere. But even new words, such as *television*, *escalator*, and *videocassette recorder*, are usually based on much older roots.

Many of those older roots come from other languages that also descended from Proto-Indo-European, languages such as Latin and ancient Greek. For explorers of English, one ancient language is of particular interest. It was a language spoken by tribes of people who once lived in parts of present-day Germany, Holland, and Scandinavia. Those tribes invaded the island of Britain in the fifth century A.D. They conquered the Britons, who were living there. The invaders brought their language to Britain. And that language was to become English.

I
The History of English
Begins with English History

". . . We shall go on to the end . . . We shall fight with growing confidence and growing strength in the air, we shall defend our island, whatever the cost may be. We shall fight on the beaches, we shall fight on the landing grounds, we shall fight in the fields and in the streets, we shall fight in the hills; we shall never surrender. . . ."

WINSTON CHURCHILL, *1940*

Those stirring words were spoken by one of the great masters of the English language. Winston Churchill led the British people during World War II, and in those terrifying times, he rallied and comforted them. When Churchill spoke of defending "our island," he meant Britain, the island in the North Atlantic that is home to England, Scotland, and Wales. In 1940, enemy forces from Germany were overpowering the nations of Europe. The Germans planned to invade Britain and conquer the British people.

It was not the first time that the island had been threatened with invasion from the European continent. It had even faced the same threat from the Germans earlier in the same century, during World War I. As it turned out, the Germans never made it across the sea during either world war. The inhabitants of the island remained free. But it was not always so.

Throughout history, the island now known as Great Britain was invaded and settled, invaded and settled. Once, long ago, invaders from what is now Germany *were* successful in conquering the island. If they, like the modern Germans, had failed, the history of England and the world would have been quite different. For one thing, the English language as we know it would not exist. But the story starts even earlier, with a different invasion.

Old English

In the first century A.D., invading armies from Rome succeeded in conquering much of Britain. The Romans, extending their vast empire westward, turned their part of the island into a Roman province by A.D. 80. They called the province Britannia, borrowing the island natives' own name for themselves, Britons. The Britons spoke Celtic, the Romans spoke Latin, and the two languages were spoken side by side for the entire period of Roman rule. Four hundred years!

The Romans brought with them the most up-to-date civilization of the time. They built towns, roads, buildings, fortifications, and splendid baths. They introduced a system of writing and an organized government. In later years, they brought Christianity to the Britons. Over the many generations of

10

Roman occupation, the conquered people of Britannia came to think of themselves not as conquered people but as Romans.

Then, in the early 400's, the Roman governors and armies departed. They went off to try to rescue what remained of the crumbling Roman Empire. Britannia was now abandoned. It was no longer a protected province of Rome.

The times turned violent. Slave raiders attacked from the northern part of the island and from the west. Pirates attacked from the east. The Roman system of government broke apart. British chieftains claimed separate territories. They fought against one another. Instead of uniting the island, they divided it. Unrest and bloodshed were the result.

Across the sea to the east were tribes of people who saw opportunity in Britannia. The men were warriors and sailors, proud of their fighting skills. Eager to prove themselves in battle, they willingly followed their leaders anywhere and obeyed them until the moment of death.

These fierce people lived on the coastlands of northern Europe, but they desired new and better lands. They knew of the rich pastureland on the island of Britannia. They knew of the woods full of timber for building. They knew of those things because many of their own men had served as soldiers in the Roman armies in Britannia and had settled there generations earlier. And even long before that, these Germanic people had periodically sailed across the North Sea to stage pirate raids along the east coast of the island. They knew it was time to invade.

The Germanic invaders, tribes known as Angles, Saxons,

and Jutes, did not succeed in conquering Britannia all at once. They planned a quick and powerful invasion, but it failed. The Britons managed to drive them back. Not for long, however.

The tribes moved in gradually. Slowly they took over the island. Where they met resistance from the Britons, they battled. The Germanic tribes also fought each other for territory. The island was torn apart by war for hundreds of years.

The famous legends of King Arthur and the Knights of the Round Table are based on events in this period of British history. It was said that Arthur, a Briton, managed to unite the quarreling British factions and defeat the invaders, for a while. Many historians believe that there really was such a leader, even though the details of his life are unknown. The tales told about Arthur are mostly myths.

True or not, the tales have lasted a long time. Even today, stories are written and movies made that tell of King Arthur, the spell-casting magician Merlin, the fair queen Guinevere, the famous knight Sir Launcelot, and the magnificent city where Arthur made his home, Camelot.

But neither Arthur nor any other British leader was able to stop the invaders from taking British land and holding it. The Germanic invaders set up separate kingdoms on the island. By that time, the British leaders had been killed. Other Britons had fled across the sea to what is now Brittany, in France. Many escaped by heading north and west to Scotland and Wales. Others were enslaved by the conquerors. Some Britons remained. But their language traveled elsewhere.

Celtic, the language spoken by the native Britons, disappeared from the areas of Germanic settlement. Celtic was the original language of England, but it played almost no role in the history of the English language. All that is left to us from the original Celtic vocabulary is a handful of infrequently used words. Some describe elements of the landscape, such as *crag* (a steep, rugged rock forming part of a cliff) and *tor* (a pile of rocks on a hill); and others appear in modern place names, such as *Avon*, the Celtic word for "water," and *Bryn Mawr*, "great hill." Celtic was replaced by the language spoken by the Germanic conquerors.

Generations passed. The children of the great-grandchildren of the wild sea warriors were now farmers and shepherds. Time and distance had changed their language. It was different from the one spoken back in northern Europe. By A.D. 700, the settlers were calling their language by a new name—*Englisc*. (The sound spelled *sc* is like our modern *sh*.)

The Germanic tribes who set up kingdoms on the conquered island have come to be known as Anglo-Saxons. Their language is today called Old English. In a variety of forms, Old English was spoken for hundreds of years.

The early Anglo-Saxons were mostly illiterate. Like many peoples who did not read or write, they had a strong oral tradition. Their singers and storytellers passed along the legends and histories of their people from one generation to the next. Every generation learned the tales by listening and by memorizing.

They were rich tales of heroes and danger. In the halls of the Anglo-Saxon kings, a singer would pluck a harp and recite the story of the courageous warrior-king Beowulf and the murdering monster Grendel who could not be defeated by human weapons. Beowulf wrestled with Grendel and ripped the arm right out of the beast's shoulder.

The poem that told of Beowulf's exploits against monsters and a dragon was a rousing one that took three hours to tell. It is the most famous example of Old English poetry, a masterpiece that is still studied in literature classes. We know about *Beowulf* because it and other Old English poems and stories were eventually written down.

Old English was written with a borrowed alphabet used by the only people who knew how to write in those times — Christian priests, monks, and nuns. The alphabet they borrowed was the Roman one. That was the alphabet they had learned to use to write Latin, which was the language of the Roman Catholic Church.

The Roman alphabet used by the Christian scribes had twenty-three letters. (You would recognize those letters easily. You are looking at updated examples of them right now.) The letters represented the sounds spoken in Old English words. The scribes added extra symbols to stand for sounds not heard in Latin and therefore not represented by Roman letters. Symbols called a thorn þ and an eth ð were used to spell the *th* sounds heard in *path* and *then.* And the short *a* vowel sound heard in *cat* was spelled æ. Thus, the word spelled þæt in Old English would be our modern word *that.*

The Old English word *cniht* meant "boy" or "youth" and was pronounced "kneeht" — with the *k* and the *h* sounded.

(That *h* sound is no longer part of English. It was somewhat like the sound you hear at the beginning of *huge,* if you exaggerate it.) The Anglo-Saxons pronounced a sound for every letter of the word *cniht,* but in our modern spelling of the same word, *knight,* sounds for three letters, *k, g,* and *h,* are not heard.

Such so-called silent letters are everywhere in modern English words, often causing mischief for spellers. These letters came to us from Old English ones that were, in fact, pronounced. Just as we make sounds for both consonants in **cl**ub and **dr**ive, the Anglo-Saxons pronounced both consonants at the start of **wr**ist, **sw**ord (written in Old English as *sweord*), **kn**ife (in Old English, *cnif*), and **gn**at (in Old English, *gnæt*).

The Anglo-Saxons also pronounced consonant combinations that our English-speaking mouths would find tricky to produce—Old English words began with combinations such as *fn, hl, hr, wl,* and *hw.* (The *hw* combination has been passed down to modern English, but we spell it *wh,* and many of us no longer pronounce the *h.*) Look at the two Old English words below.

hwæt   hwæðer

They may seem odd at first, but if you think about the information in the four paragraphs before them, you may be able to figure out the modern English versions. (For the answer, find the * at the bottom of the page.)

Even though the English we speak today is descended

* The two words in modern English are *what* and *whether.*

15

from the language spoken by the Anglo-Saxons, Old English is quite different from modern English. It must be studied like a foreign language. Yet many connections between old and new can be seen and heard.

Take the days of the week, for example. The early Anglo-Saxon kings, who had the complete devotion of the warriors they commanded, all claimed to be descended from gods. Most claimed descent from Woden, who was the most important and powerful of the gods. Originally written as *Wodnes dæg*, the "day of Woden" is now known as Wednesday. The day that the Anglo-Saxons set aside for the god of war, Tiw (or Tiu), was *Tiwes dæg* — Tuesday. The wife of Woden, Frigga, had a day too — *Frigedæg*, now called Friday. The day belonging to the god of thunder, Thunor, is now called Thursday, and the name of the Roman god Saturn was borrowed for Saturday. *Sunday* and *Monday* come from Old English words for "sun" and "moon."

The Anglo-Saxons held onto their worship of gods for more than a hundred years after their arrival in Britain. When they converted to Christianity (by the middle of the seventh century), many of their original religious customs became part of the new Christian observances. These customs have been passed down to us.

The Anglo-Saxons worshipped a goddess named Eostre and held a spring festival in her honor. Today the goddess is no longer known, and *Easter* is a Christian holiday observed in the spring. *Yule*, which refers to Christmas or the Christmas season (the yule log is still a popular fireplace item), was originally a twelve-day Anglo-Saxon festival at which animals were sacrificed to the gods. Fifteen hundred years have passed since the twelve days of Yule were observed; Christians now observe the twelve days of Christmas instead.

The Anglo-Saxons had firm beliefs in the supernatural—in vengeful gods and devils. Dragons and other beasts that appear in modern children's stories bear a strong resemblance to the creatures that played important roles in the folklore of the Anglo-Saxons. One supernatural creature, a demon called *mare*, took its victims while they were sleeping. It's easy to see why a horrifying dream is given the name *nightmare*. (And now you also know why the *mare* in the word has nothing to do with a female horse. The Anglo-Saxon word for a female horse was *mearh*.)

From Old English words for "man," *wer*, and "wolf," *wulf*, the Anglo-Saxons' *werwulf* has become that familiar horror-movie howler, the werewolf.

Most of the words used by speakers of Old English have not been passed down to us. Estimates are that eighty-five percent of the vocabulary of Old English never made it into modern English. The words that were passed down, however, were not limited to names for gods and monsters. In a way, we speak and write Old English every time we put words together. As a matter of fact, the sentence before this one is made entirely of words that come from Old English. The words we use most often—important little words like *the*, *and*, *for*, *of*, *here*, *like*, *think*, *run*, and *word* itself—were also spoken (in their earlier forms, naturally) by the descendants

17

of the Anglo-Saxon warriors who settled in Britain fifteen hundred years ago.

Scholars have studied all the Old English writings that have survived the centuries. They have a fairly good idea of what the language sounded like. These scholars have made recordings of Old English poems and songs. By listening to those records, you may notice that Old English does *seem* similar to modern English. Of course, most of the vocabulary and some of the sounds are not familiar to modern ears.

The first poem we know of written in Old English is "Caedmon's Hymn." Caedmon was an uneducated peasant herdsman who lived in the 600's. He is often described as the first English poet. According to later accounts, Caedmon's poem came to him in a dream, when he was directed to sing of Creation. Here are the first two lines of the very first English poem, written thirteen hundred years ago.

Nu sculon herian heofon-rices Weard
Meotodes meahte and his mod-geþ anc.

Stumped? Aside from *and* and *his*, the words are unfamiliar. Translated into a less rhythmical modern English version, the lines become

Now we shall praise the Guardian of the heavenly kingdom,
The might of the Creator and his thoughts.

Now you may be able to see a few more connections: *now* and *nu*, *might* and *meahte*, *heaven* and *heofon*. But as you

18

can tell, the road from Old English to modern English still needed to be traveled. At the start of the road, taking the first few steps, were the Anglo-Saxons. What were they like, these speakers of a language they called Englisc?

The Anglo-Saxons

The Anglo-Saxon settlers were unlike the Roman occupiers who had departed Britain. The Anglo-Saxons did not know what to make of the walled towns built by the Romans. They preferred to live in rural villages. They cleared woodlands to create fields for farming and for raising livestock. They used the timber to build protective stockades around their villages. They also used it for their homes. Anglo-Saxon dwellings were made of wood, thatch, twigs, and mud. The simplest ones were sunken huts, with earthen floors dug two feet underground and with thatched sides shaped like a tent. Other Anglo-Saxons lived in barnlike wooden structures — families at one end, cattle at the other. Since indoor fires were used for warmth and cooking, these wooden homes were always in danger of burning. By Roman standards, Anglo-Saxon living conditions were primitive, even squalid. The Romans, after all, had built grand public baths in Britain. Wealthy families in Britain had been accustomed to elegant living quarters — with beautiful decorations, central heating, and private baths.

Life was hard for the Anglo-Saxon pioneers. It was especially hard for the people at the bottom of Anglo-Saxon society —

the slaves. A slave was someone captured in war, born to slave parents, or sold into slavery. A freeborn peasant facing starvation during a bad crop year, for example, might have sold a child into slavery in exchange for food.

The peasant class was made up of farmers and shepherds, along with weavers, potters, and other artisans. Beautiful jeweled objects were valued by wealthy Anglo-Saxons, and the metalworking skills of Anglo-Saxon artisans were well-known throughout Europe. Freeborn workers included those who had some property of their own as well as those who worked for masters. These free peasants were not slaves, but their freedom would seem like slavery to us. Economic choice was unknown. Peasants owed rent and service to a landowner, and they were dependent upon that landowner for help and protection. No freeborn peasant could simply pick himself up and work on a different master's land.

At the next level of society were the nobility. Most were landholders, and their dwellings of timber and thatch were larger and sturdier than the huts of the slaves and peasants. The highest-ranking nobles were the chief, or "old," men called *ealdormen,* who served the king directly. (Perhaps your town or city government includes *aldermen*; you now know where the term comes from.)

The role of the nobility was to fight the battles of the king. The king sat at the top of the social ladder, and that ladder could be shaky. The Anglo-Saxons created seven kingdoms in Britain, each with a different king. Sometimes, the kings formed alliances with one another. At other times, they battled each other for control over land.

Drawn from the different classes of Anglo-Saxon society were men and women who devoted themselves to the religious life. They lived in monasteries and convents or traveled among the people to spread the religion that was based in Rome under the leadership of the pope. That religion was Christianity.

Christianity was an important civilizing force throughout Europe during the Middle Ages. The force was felt strongly in Anglo-Saxon Britain. With Christianity came education. Monks, priests, and nuns learned to read and write Latin. They were the teachers and the preservers of knowledge. From the convents and monasteries came prized treasures—books.

The Christian scribes wrote upon parchment, paperlike sheets made by scraping, treating, and cutting animal skins to size. They shaped reeds or goose quills into pens. They gathered soot and used it to prepare ink. Then they copied—every letter, every word, slowly and carefully—by hand. No wonder books were rare items! But as Christianity spread, so did monasteries and convents. As the number of scholars and scribes grew, so grew the number of books. Christianity brought literacy to the Anglo-Saxons. It also turned Britain into a leading center of learning. All Europe knew of the great scholars and excellent libraries of Britain.

For the Anglo-Saxons, Christianity became a powerful influence. But its strength was about to be tested. How well would Christian force stand up to brute force?

Three hundred years after the arrival of their pagan sea-warrior ancestors, the Anglo-Saxon inhabitants of Britain faced a life-threatening danger: pagan sea warriors. Like the Anglo-

Saxons' own ancestors, these new sea pirates came from northern Europe. Their homelands were Norway and Denmark, and they were called Vikings. These were the same Vikings renowned for their adventurousness. They were the same Vikings who would cross the open ocean westward to reach the North American continent almost five hundred years before Columbus rediscovered it.

The Vikings were expert sailors, but their fearsome powers were not limited to the sea. They landed their ships on the English coast and descended like wolves on the countryside — stealing, burning, murdering. By the mid-800's, Viking hit-and-run attacks were becoming more and more frequent. Then, just like the invaders who had come before them, they began to set up permanent settlements.

One by one, the Anglo-Saxon kingdoms fell to the Viking victors. Finally, only one kingdom remained. It was the powerful kingdom of the West Saxons, also known as Wessex. Wessex survived because its leaders were especially strong. But in the year 871, when the Danes (the Vikings in Britain came mostly from Denmark) were pressing closer and closer, the king of Wessex died. Control of the kingdom passed to his younger brother.

The new king was only twenty-three. Luckily, he was already experienced in war. He had led Anglo-Saxon soldiers into battle against the Danes, and now he readied the noblemen and armies of Wessex for further battles. The young king's name was Alfred.

For seven years, Alfred was able to keep Wessex under

Anglo-Saxon control. Then, with a surprise attack, the Danes managed to occupy large areas of the kingdom. Alfred and a small force fled to safety.

The man who had controlled the strongest Anglo-Saxon kingdom in Britain was now hiding in the woods and marshes, cold and hungry. Alfred and his supporters had nothing to live on, except what they could capture by raiding Viking encampments or villages under Viking control.

This dismal, hopeless period of English history inspired later storytellers to give creative accounts of King Alfred's misery. The most famous of these legends describes the king, alone and in rags, seeking shelter in the hut of a herdsman. As Alfred sits by the fire, the herdsman's wife, not knowing the identity of her guest, scolds the king for allowing loaves of bread to burn in the oven. Imagine how low the poor king's fortunes had sunk—that he should be reprimanded by a herdsman's wife for not helping with the household chores!

In spite of hardships, Alfred planned and directed the building of fortifications. From his stronghold, he attacked the Danes. The people of Wessex, who had feared that their king was dead, were now heartened and joined in the struggle. The Anglo-Saxons forced the Viking armies to retreat. Alfred won back his kingdom.

Alfred knew that the Danes never gave up easily. He suspected that their defeat was only temporary. He commanded that a system of defense works be built throughout the countryside to protect the kingdom from further attacks.

Years later, when the Danes returned to try to take control of Wessex again, they were unable to penetrate the Anglo-Saxon defenses. Alfred even managed to defeat the Danes in their own element—the sea. In longboats of Alfred's own design, his sailors battled the Danes and won.

In the difficult times of the Danish invasions, the Anglo-Saxons were lucky to have a leader like Alfred, someone who could plan, organize, and take action. Alfred was, without a doubt, a brilliant military strategist. But other men of his time had noteworthy military talents, and their names are nearly forgotten. Why is it that Alfred is still a well-known hero, even though more than one thousand years have passed since his death? The answer is that Alfred did much more for Britain than win battles.

To us, it may seem strange that someone living way back in the 800's would long for "the good old days," but that is exactly the way Alfred felt. Despite his military skill and success, Alfred wished for peace and for the good things that can come with peace. A century before him, Britain had been a great center of learning and religion. But with the Danes had come the destruction of churches. The libraries within them had also been destroyed. Religious leaders and teachers lost their influence. By Alfred's time, literacy was no longer widespread. Alfred himself, the son of a king, had not learned to read English until he was twelve. He was also unable to read Latin, the language of religion, scholarship, and books. Alfred feared that no one else in his kingdom could read Latin either. He was deeply troubled by the loss of learning in a land that had once been such a vital center of scholarship. He decided to make some changes.

Alfred sent messengers and gifts to religious leaders in various parts of Britain and in Europe. He wanted these leaders to send learned men to Wessex to revive religion and education. Many of his requests were granted, and scholars came to Alfred's kingdom. They came to teach, to set up new religious centers, and to help Alfred with the next stage of his plan.

Alfred selected those written works that he believed were "most necessary for all men to know." These books were written in Latin, of course, a language that Alfred could now read and understand—with the help of the learned teachers in his court. It seemed to Alfred that important books should be translated "into the language that we can all understand." That language was Old English.

Alfred wanted literacy to spread. He sensed that more people would learn to read if they were taught in the language they already knew how to speak. The idea seems simple and obvious, doesn't it? Alfred was the first to think of it.

For the first time, Latin works were translated (several by Alfred himself) into the language of the Anglo-Saxon people. Alfred used those works in the program of education he started. He wrote that all freeborn young men should be set to learning "until the time that they can read English writings properly."

It was the young men whom Alfred wanted to educate. What about the young women? Compared with women in other societies of the time, Anglo-Saxon women had advantages. Some were able to rise to positions of political and religious influence—Alfred's own daughter was to become a capable and respected leader. But most girls were not given the same opportunities granted to their brothers.

Alfred wanted the future leaders of his kingdom to be literate. Through the study of wisdom, Alfred believed, the officials of government could become wise. The place to start was right in his royal household. Alfred set up a school where his own children could be educated along with the sons of the nobility.

It was one thing to require the sons of leaders to read, write, and think. It was quite another to demand that their fathers learn too. But that is precisely what Alfred demanded. He warned that if the officials of his government did not learn to read (or show that they were trying with all their might to learn), they must give up their official duties. Alfred's message was clear: Read, or else!

A member of Alfred's court reported that there was quite a bit of sighing as these powerful leaders struggled to learn to read. It is not known how many succeeded.

Still, the results of Alfred's efforts could be seen even in his own lifetime. The standards of religion and education were raised. Official business began to be recorded in writing. Churches multiplied. Libraries began to grow. New and beautifully decorated manuscripts were created.

What else did Alfred accomplish? He presented a legal code in which he specified and explained ideas of justice.

During his reign, a plan was set in motion for a written history of the Anglo-Saxon people. That history, now known as *The Anglo-Saxon Chronicle*, includes accounts of important events. It is a source still studied by grateful historians.

Under Alfred's strong leadership, a feeling of unity spread among the Anglo-Saxons. Their land was becoming a single nation. Soon a new name for the nation, based on the name of the tribe called the Angles, would appear in written records: Englaland.

King Alfred ruled during a time of invasions and threatened invasions, always preoccupied with the security of his kingdom. Yet he valued peace, religion, justice, and learning. He acted to bring those values to his people. Alfred's achievements seem superhuman when you consider that Alfred did not have good health and struggled with episodes of serious physical pain. Perhaps his suffering was due to a stomach or intestinal disease; the exact nature of his illness is a mystery. Medicine was an undeveloped science during the Middle Ages, and Alfred could not be cured.

Six hundred years after Alfred's death, historians began to realize how truly outstanding Alfred's qualities and achievements were. They began to write *the Great* after his name. Of all the kings and queens who have ruled England, only one has been given that special honor. He is the Anglo-Saxon king Alfred the Great.

Thanks to Alfred's efforts to provide books in English for his people, modern scholars have many examples of Old

English writings to study. These language scholars have compared Alfred's translations to the Latin originals. They have examined Old English works like "Caedmon's Hymn" and *Beowulf* and *The Anglo-Saxon Chronicle*. They have learned how Old English was like the language we now call English and how it was different. They have explained (and continue to explain) the kinds of changes that the language underwent as it traveled from then to now. Changes were already taking place in King Alfred's time. Some of those changes involved the Danes who had settled in the northern and eastern portions of England.

Languages Apart and Together

Anglo-Saxons continued to live in the regions controlled by the Danes. The Danes had settled down as farmers, shepherds, and traders, and they lived peacefully beside their Anglo-Saxon neighbors. As the decades passed, Anglo-Saxons and Danes began conducting business with each other. Danish sons married Anglo-Saxon daughters, and Anglo-Saxon sons married Danish daughters. The children of those unions were Anglo-Danes, with loyalties to both groups. The two peoples were slowly merging, and so were their languages.

The Danish settlers eventually adopted Old English as their language. But they influenced the way it was spoken. The original language of the Danish settlers is today known as Old Norse. It had arisen in northern Europe, in the same region that had produced the language of the original Anglo-

Saxon invaders. Because the two languages had similar points of origin, speakers of Old Norse and speakers of Old English could understand each other.

The languages had similar vocabularies. Both groups used the words *man*, *mother*, *house*, *life*, *come*, *bring*, *see*, and *think*, for example. Each group may have thought the other was speaking with a funny accent, however, since their pronunciations differed. The two languages also had differences in grammar.

The grammar of a language describes the ways sentences are put together to give meaning. In modern English, the sentence "The child hit the ball" is entirely different in meaning from "The ball hit the child." In modern English, word order makes all the difference.

In Old English, word order didn't matter so much. What mattered more were the special endings added to words to identify who or what did the hitting and who or what was being hit.

Take the name for a male child, for example. In modern English, it is *son*; in Old English, *sunu*. Today we add just one ending (spelled *s* or *'s*) to mean "more than one son" or "belonging to the son": "her three *sons*" or "that *son's* house." Old English speakers attached many other endings. Depending on how the word worked in the sentence, they would say *sunu* or *suniu* or *suna* or *sunum*. And other kinds of words required other endings.

Danish speakers of Old Norse also added endings to their words. But theirs were slightly different from the ones used by their Anglo-Saxon neighbors. Over time, as the two groups mingled, they found themselves dropping some of their endings altogether. They were changing the grammar of Old English.

As the Danes became speakers of Old English, they made other changes in its grammar and its vocabulary. Our modern pronouns *they*, *them*, and *their*, and the verb *are* — as well as the helpful expression *the same* — all come from the Danes. They contributed well over one thousand new words, including such common ones as *guess*, *sister*, *wrong*, *get*, *die*, *anger*, and *take*. It's not that the Anglo-Saxons had no words for such basic concepts; it's that the Old Norse version of the word replaced the Old English version.

Old English speakers used the word *niman* to mean "to get hold of." The Old Norse word was *taka*, and that version is the one that survived — as our modern verb *to take*. A similar pattern is seen with the word *window*, which comes from an Old Norse word meaning "wind-eye." The Anglo-Saxons' name for a window was *eye-thirl*. (The Old English word *thirl* meant "hole"; it still appears in the second syllable of our word for a nose hole, *nostril*.)

Like their Anglo-Saxon neighbors, the Danes kept slaves. In Old English, the word for "slave" was *theow*. In Old Norse, it was *thrall*. Have you ever been so *enthralled* by something that you could not break free? Only the Old Norse word has been passed down to us.

Even though Old Norse words sometimes replaced the Old English versions, it was actually more common for Old English and Old Norse words to survive together. That is one reason modern English has such a rich supply of words with similar meanings, or synonyms. The Danes gave us *skill*, the Anglo-Saxons gave us *craft*. The Danes spoke of an animal's *skin*, the Anglo-Saxons of its *hide*. The Danes had *law* on their side; the Anglo-Saxons claimed *right*.

Synonyms inherited from Old English and Old Norse may have closely related meanings, or they may have distinctly different meanings. From Old Norse we have the word *die*. The Old English version of "to die" was *steorfan*. Over time the Old English word came to refer only to a slow death, the kind of dying that results from disease, cold, or hunger. After that the word took on an even more specific meaning. Today one form of the Old English word is heard in familiar expressions like this: "Have you got anything to eat? I'm *starving!*"

One way to spot a word that comes from Old Norse is to listen for the sound that is often spelled *sk*, as in *sky*. The Anglo-Saxons did not use that combination of consonant sounds, so its presence is a signal that Danes were doing the talking. Words such as *sky*, *scare*, *skin*, and *skill* were added to Old English in the days when Anglo-Saxons and Danes lived side by side in England.

Generations passed. The time was now the eleventh century. The place was England, a single nation under the leadership of a king and powerful noblemen called earls. The people were Anglo-Saxons, Danes, and Anglo-Danes. The groups were living peaceably. But the history of England, as you must realize by now, is a history of invasions. Permanent peace was not possible. Who would the next invaders be?

Back in the time of King Alfred, England was not the only victim of Viking terrorists. All of Europe suffered under the swords of the wild men from the north. A Viking chief named Rollo had led a band of followers into the kingdom of France. They had settled on land on the northwestern shore. This region of France, the land of the Northmen, became known as Normandy, and the descendants of the Viking settlers were called Normans. Normandy was a part of France, a political unit called a duchy. The duchy of Normandy was ruled by a series of dukes descended from Rollo.

Just as the Vikings in England had adopted the language of England, the Normans had adopted the language of France. They spoke Norman French, a variety of Old French. Unlike Old English, which was based on a Germanic language, Old French was based on Latin.

The Normans adopted more than a language from their French neighbors. They also borrowed the Christian religion, a legal system, and a form of government. They borrowed a whole social structure, in fact, in which vast power and wealth were concentrated in the hands of just a few men.

In the middle of the eleventh century, that power and wealth had come into the hands of William, duke of Normandy. Duke William's eyes, however, looked beyond Normandy. To England. William wanted the English throne. He had been promised it by the English king. William was distantly related to the king of England. His wife was even a descendant of Alfred. William was determined: The English throne would someday be his.

At the time, England was ruled by a great-great-great-grandson of Alfred. This king's mother was Norman, and he had spent half his life in Normandy. The king's name was Edward, though he was later to be known as Edward the Confessor. It was his saintlike piety that earned him his nickname. Possibly because of his religious preoccupations, King Edward was a weak ruler. Much power rested with the English earls, who ruled the four major provinces of England. Edward also had no children, so when he died in 1066, he left no heirs. In the Middle Ages, the death of a king without heirs was a signal for turmoil.

The death of the king. No royal son to inherit the throne. Powerful English earls. Put those elements together, and what do you get? Earl Harold Godwineson, the earl of Wessex, was crowned king of England immediately after Edward's death. It was not a promising event. The skies were not clear.

The skies were literally not clear, in fact. Halley's Comet was making an appearance in that spring of 1066. Everyone looked up at it with terror. People in those times were superstitious. To them omens and evil magic were facts, not myth. The people of England were sure that this fiery visitor in the sky was bringing a message of doom. They were certain that something awful was about to happen. They were right.

Across the Channel, Duke William of Normandy learned

that Harold had been crowned king. He was outraged. This upstart earl with barely a drop of royal blood had no claim to his—William's—throne! Years before, Harold had sworn an oath of loyalty to William. And now he had broken that oath. What treachery!

William immediately began to raise an army and to build the ships that would carry men and horses to England. Harold Godwineson would have to defend his throne.

Earl Harold Godwineson believed he had the right to the English throne. He was a capable and commanding leader. His sister had been married to King Edward. On his deathbed, Edward had named Harold as his successor. It was true that Harold had almost no royal blood, but at least he had *English* blood. Duke William was French.

To make matters worse, another claimant was preparing to take the English throne by force. This claimant wasn't English either. He was the king of Norway, a towering warrior called Harald Hardrada. While Duke William was assembling his troops in Normandy, Harald Hardrada set sail for England with his army.

The brand-new king of England, Harold, marched north with his English army to meet the forces of Harald Hardrada. In the battle that followed, the king of Norway and most of his soldiers were killed. Elated by his victory, the English Harold marched two hundred miles back to London. There he learned that William of Normandy was on the way.

There was no time to waste. English survivors of the battle against Harald Hardrada were gathered together, along with new troops hastily assembled in London. There were perhaps seven thousand fighters in all, noblemen and peasants, now marching east to meet the Norman invaders.

Exhausted by two weeks of fighting and marching, Harold and his troops made camp the day before the battle. Still, they were eager for another victory. They readied their spears, shields, swords, and battle-axes. It was Friday the thirteenth.

By the end of the next day, most of the English, including Harold, lay dead.

William, duke of Normandy, was the victor that day at the famous Battle of Hastings. His Norman archers had broken through the wall of shields held by the English defenders. His Norman cavalry had cut down the English foot soldiers.

The immediate result of William's victory was that he could now prepare to have himself crowned king of England. There were other results—far-reaching ones. William the Conqueror's victory at the Battle of Hastings, October 14, 1066, changed the history of the English people. It also changed the history of their language.

William the Conqueror was a shrewd and skillful ruler. He knew how to get power, and he knew how to hold on to it: with cruelty.

In return for the Norman nobility's helping him gain the English throne, William gave them English lands. He started by confiscating all the property of any Englishman who had fought on Harold's side at Hastings. He continued by killing nearly all the English nobles who were left.

The English people did not consent easily to being ruled

by foreigners. There was resistance—skirmishing against the Norman nobles as they moved into their new estates. William squashed English rebellion in the north by marching there with his Norman troops, killing any English men and boys he found along the way. When he reached the regions that harbored the resisters, he ordered that all the grain, cattle, and farming equipment be gathered together in heaps and burned. Then he marched back, leaving the people of those regions to face famine and death.

William also brought in Normans to replace the English heads of churches. The English monks at one church decided they would not obey their Norman leader. They refused to substitute Norman chants and ceremonies for the ones they loved. Norman archers were called in to teach the monks a lesson. The archers chased the monks into the church and used them for target practice.

The Norman settlers were greatly outnumbered by the people they ruled. To maintain control, they used terror. Punishment for disobedience was harsh: blinding, torture, mutilation, hanging. One of William's sons restored value to the coins of his realm by cutting off the right hands of all the moneyers who were minting coins illegally.

The Norman rulers also decreed that all forestlands—vast regions of the countryside, some inhabited—belonged to the king. Only the royal foresters were permitted to hunt boar or deer or to set traps for game. The forests of England became the private hunting grounds of the Norman kings. That meant, of course, that the English people could not hunt for meat in their own homeland. If they were caught, they were maimed or killed. Later these bitter punishments were replaced with fines, which became a regular source of income for the nobility.

The English people never abandoned their forests, despite the risks. Eventually English hunters developed such skill with a new weapon, the longbow, that their fame spread throughout Europe. In later times, no army could defeat an army made up of English archers. Among the users of the longbow was an outlaw known as Robin Hood, who lived in Sherwood Forest with his companions and built a reputation for stealing from the rich and giving to the poor. This hero of the Middle Ages may not have been a real person at all. Ballad makers may have invented Robin Hood, responding to the English people's great need for a hero with moral courage. Such heroes, whether real or fictional, often emerge during difficult times.

The Norman kings believed they were entitled to all the forests of England. They believed they were entitled to all the land, as a matter of fact. The Normans planned to establish in England the same economic, social, and political system that was in place throughout Europe during the Middle Ages. The system was feudalism; *feud* meant "estate." In a feudal society, land could be granted in return for pledges of service. The king owned all property, either outright or through his nobles.

With feudalism came knights and the ideals of knighthood. William the Conqueror's knights on horseback were called chevaliers, "men on horses." A related word, *chivalry*, still expresses the ideals of bravery, gallantry, and loyalty associated with the knights of the Middle Ages.

With feudalism came the abolishment of slavery in England. Slaves were replaced, however, with a new lowest class. The English free peasant became unfree and was now required to serve a lord. These peasants of reduced status were called villeins. Today speakers of English may call a base scoundrel by the name *villain*. The original villains (or villeins) may not have been scoundrels, but their station in life was certainly base.

The Normans also imported new building techniques. Within weeks after the Battle of Hastings, they had constructed wooden towers on earth mounds. They soon began to replace these temporary fortresses with massive defensive structures of stone. The private strongholds of the Norman nobles had great halls, towers, battlements, and moats; they are the buildings that most of us picture when we hear their name: *castles*. The Normans built castles by the hundreds.

A new ruling class. Feudalism. Architecture. These were major Norman changes, but not the only changes. The Norman conquerors brought something else to England: their language.

The Normans who settled in England were not like the previous invaders, the Danes and Anglo-Saxons. The Normans were rulers. They did not mingle with the common people. William the Conqueror made an effort to learn English so that he could speak to his new subjects. He did not have the time for proper study, however, and he remained largely ignorant of the language of the people he ruled.

For generations the king and nobles of England spoke French. They traveled between their estates in France and those in England, and they thought of themselves as French. King Henry II, who ruled from 1133 to 1189, spent only thirteen of those years in England. His son King Richard I also spent little time in England. King Richard's adviser, a power-hungry man named Longchamp, grabbed so much control that he was practically ruling England in the king's absence. Eventually Longchamp's dictatorial practices were his undoing. Forced to flee England for his life, Longchamp disguised himself as an English peasant woman peddling rolls of cloth under her arm. A group of real peasant women spotted this peddler and began to question her about her wares. Strangely enough, this peddler spoke no English! Longchamp soon had the veil torn from his face. Found out because he tried to rule the land without ever learning the language of its people!

Shortly after William the Conqueror came to power, the written language of government changed from Old English to Latin. This was another custom imported from France, where government documents and orders were recorded in Latin. Latin was also the language of learning, which was largely the domain of the Church. Norman history was recorded in Latin too.

The French language also began to be used in official documents. It became the language of the law courts.

What happened to Old English writings? Written examples from the period after the Norman invasion are rare. The last entry in a copy of *The Anglo-Saxon Chronicle* is dated

1154. The few Old English writings that have survived are mostly religious lessons for the poor.

Old English was no longer the language of the powerful, so it was no longer worth recording. As an oral language, however, Old English thrived. It was the language of the people. Their rulers may have favored French, but the English people — the peasants, tradespeople, artisans — continued to speak English. Largely illiterate, these people were unconcerned with establishing any proper or literary standards for English. They simply said what they meant. For about two hundred years after the Norman Conquest, the English language traveled and grew and changed among the plain folk, who neither read nor wrote it.

The speakers of Old English continued to drop the special endings that were attached to words and to let word order give the meaning instead. And the range of possible answers to the question Which ones? was gradually reduced from eighteen different words to just five: *the*, *that*, *this*, *these*, *those*.

English speakers also made past-tense verbs more regular. Just as a child learning English today may attach *-ed* to fit a pattern, as in "The dog *runned* away" or "I *eated* it all up," speakers of Old English used similar reasoning to alter verb forms. Past-tense forms such as *clomb* (rhymed with *home*), *bearn*, *holp*, *stop* (rhymed with *hope*), and *welk* slowly changed into their modern forms: *climbed*, *burned*, *helped*, *stepped*, and *walked*.

Some of those past-tense forms were not changed, which is why we say "I ran" (not "runned"), "I ate" (not "eated"), "I gave" (not "gived"), and "I brought" (not "bringed").

Some verbs changed, some didn't, and some are still in between, as you can tell by these two equally correct sentences:

"I *dreamed* about you last night."
"Really? I *dreamt* about you too!"

Members of the ruling class may have been slow to pick up English, but those English people who served them began to pick up French. English farmers continued to tend their animals and to call them by their Old English names. When English servants delivered these animals to the French nobles' tables, however, French names were used. In modern English, that difference is preserved. A twelfth-century English farmer spoke of the *cow*, *calf*, *sheep*, or *swine*. The English servant delivered the meats on French platters as *beef, veal, mutton,* and *bacon* (or *pork*).

Then, as now, the French prided themselves on their appreciation of good food. French words were added to the vocabulary of the English people who labored in the nobles' kitchens and dining halls: *Roast, gravy, fry,* and *jelly* have all come into English from Old French.

More than nine hundred years later, speakers of English still find that French food-and-cooking terms have a superior flavor. Even the humblest roadside diner may offer the "soup of the day" as *soupe du jour*. A *chef* and a *cook* may prepare food equally well, but a head cook working at a fine restaurant prefers the French title of *chef*. Vegetables will taste the same whether you *pan-fry* or *sauté* them, but cookbooks almost always recommend that you sauté: Doing it the French way somehow sounds more elegant.

Other French words trickled into the English vocabulary as English natives came into contact with their Norman masters in other ways. English churchgoers began to use the French terms *baptism*, *sermon*, and *pray*. English messengers picked up words used in the law courts, where business was conducted in French: *judge*, *jury*, *marry*, *robber*. French words that described the imported architecture began to pass English lips: *palace*, *castle*, *beauty*, *art*. Since the immigrants were wealthy landowners, they had time for entertainment. Such words as *joy*, *delight*, *comfort*, *sport*, and *pleasure* became part of the vocabulary of their hardworking servants.

As time passed, more and more English speakers became bilingual. Most peasants got along perfectly well speaking only English, but knowledge of French was a necessity for anyone who did business with the upper classes. No one can tell now, but England might have become a permanently bilingual nation, or perhaps even a French-speaking nation, if it had not been for a series of events that began with a particularly bad king.

King John was such a bad king that no English king since his time has ever been named John. History has been most unkind to John; he was probably not the worst king that England ever had. But there is no doubt he was a cruel tyrant. What's more, he was a failure in the attempt to hold on to his French lands. Philip II, king of France, took Normandy away from John in 1204. No longer could the king of England also be the duke of Normandy. By 1206, John had lost other possessions in France as well. The nobles with estates in both England and France were forced to decide on a place to settle. Many chose England.

Living permanently in England, with their close ties to France now broken, the nobility began to adopt the English language. The shift from French to English actually became a symbol of national pride. During the period known as the Hundred Years' War, from 1337 to 1453, England and France were continually battling. To the people of England, French had become the language of the enemy. English, the language of the common people, was now preferred.

Another force worked to make English the language of the land. England suffered tragically during the Great Plague, or Black Death, which began in 1348 and lasted two years. Half the nation died from disease. Barely enough people were left to do the necessary work of farming, building, and trading. Those laborers who survived were in such short supply that their social position rose. The language of this new rising class was, of course, English.

As the upper classes adopted English, they often found themselves struggling to find the right word. When an English word did not come to mind quickly, they used a French one instead. French words began to flood into English. By the time the upper classes were fully English-speaking, about ten thousand French words had entered English. More than seven thousand of those are still with us today.

In the year 1362, an Act of Parliament made English the official language of law. But the English of 1362 would have sounded like a foreign language to King Alfred. It was not even the same English spoken at the time of William the Conqueror. It was not Old English anymore. It had taken a new route among the Anglo-Saxons, Anglo-Danes, and Anglo-Normans who populated the unified nation of England. The language had become what we call Middle English.

II

From Middle English to Modern English

The Father of English Poetry

"Go, litel book, go, litel myn tragedye. . . ."

That line introduces the final section of a long poem called *Troilus and Criseyde*. The poem, which tells the tragic story of a doomed love affair, was written in English in the early 1380's. The poet was Geoffrey Chaucer. Chaucer wrote at a time when the English language was rapidly changing. It was the language period now known as Middle English. Chaucer himself knew that English, particularly in its written form, did not have a solid footing. After sending off his work with a gentle nudge (the modern form of the opening line above is "Go, little book, go, my little tragedy"), Chaucer expresses some fears about its future:

> *And for ther is so gret diversite*
> *In Englissh and in writyng of oure tonge,*

So prey I God that non myswrite the,
Ne the mysmetre for defaute of tonge.

A more modern English version:

And because there is such great diversity
In English and in writing of our tongue,
So I pray God that none wrongly copy thee
Nor get thy meter wrong because of a failure of tongue.

Chaucer wished that his poetry would be read and recited just as he intended it to be. But he knew he had to rely on hope and prayer, for his version was up against the "great diversity" that was the English language of six centuries ago. Poetry was an oral art form then, and poets recited their work to audiences. Whatever written versions existed were copied by hand, and poets worried about the accuracy of the scribe's eye and ear. The writings were then passed from reader to reader. It is the copied versions of Chaucer's poetry that we know today, since none of his original manuscripts have survived the centuries.

Geoffrey Chaucer, born around 1340, was the son of a wealthy merchant. At age fourteen, Chaucer became a page in the household of the daughter-in-law of King Edward III. By the time he was seventeen, he had served in the king's army and had been captured and held prisoner in France. After his ransom was paid (ransoms for prisoners of war were standard medieval practice), Chaucer returned to

England to spend most of the rest of his life as a royal courtier. He served as the king's emissary to Italy, France, and Flanders (a medieval country on the North Sea). He was appointed customs officer supervising trade in the busy port of London. He held other administrative posts, including clerk of the king's works (in charge of building and repairing royal properties) and deputy forester of the royal forest. He even served as a member of parliament. He spoke, read, and wrote French, Latin, Italian, and English. He met many of the powerful and famous figures of the day. He observed the intrigues and intricacies of royal politics. He had a fascinating career. And he was also a court poet.

It is because of his remarkable poetry that we remember Chaucer today, six hundred years after he stood before his royal listeners and performed for them. Centuries after his death, literary scholars looked back at the England of 1350 to 1400 and labeled that time the Period of Great Individual Writers. Geoffrey Chaucer, the greatest among those writers, was given the honorary title Father of English Poetry.

Chaucer's contributions to poetry were so notable because he chose to write in English, the language of the common people. Until his time, French was the language of courtly poetry, and French poetry styles were widely imitated. Chaucer himself probably began writing poetry in French, then translated French poems into English, and then began looking for ways to create English poetry that incorporated the special qualities of English speech. The stresses (or accented syllables) that occur naturally in spoken English are uneven, so English has a more irregular beat than French. Chaucer needed to figure out how to create an appealing and interesting meter, or pattern of stresses, that used the familiar rhythms of English.

French poetry used end rhymes, and Chaucer wanted to hold on to that form. He introduced French rhyming patterns to English poetry, telling his stories in rhyming verse.

And storytelling was, in fact, the poet's function in the Middle Ages. (Prose was not used for stories; most literary works were written as poems. Prose was reserved for straightforward material like manuals and technical reports.) Chaucer's role as poet in the royal household was to tell a story that entertained, that enlightened, that inspired with a moral message; a story that had pleasing rhythms and rhymes; a story that would make his audience sigh, weep, smile, and laugh out loud. Listening to the artful recitation of poetry brought pleasure and instruction to the nobility. They respected and rewarded gifted performers.

There is no doubt that Chaucer was gifted. He achieved recognition in his own lifetime, and his poetry is still read today.

The best known of Chaucer's surviving works is *The Canterbury Tales*, and it is probably the best loved. Chaucer worked on these tales for about fourteen years, and when he died in 1400, he had not yet completed the project. Chaucer conceived of this masterwork as a connected collection of stories told by different narrators. Each narrator was one of a large group of pilgrims traveling from London to the shrine of Saint Thomas à Becket in Canterbury. The route was a popular one among English people in the late Middle Ages. Such a pilgrimage was not just a religious observance but a social one, and an opportunity to enjoy a bit of travel.

The idea of pilgrims traveling together was thus a familiar one to Chaucer's audience. Also familiar, to the more learned among them, was the narrative device of putting together tales told by different characters. Chaucer probably borrowed that idea from continental European works he had read. The plots of the individual stories themselves were also mostly borrowed or adapted from various sources. Such borrowings were common among writers in Chaucer's day. Despite his dependence on others' ideas, Chaucer's work turned out to be highly original. For one thing, it was written in a language not considered literary—English. And Chaucer used an abundant array of English, from the lofty speech of the Knight, who tells an ancient tale of chivalry, to the vulgar language of the drunken Miller, who tells a bawdy (and hilarious) tale. *The Canterbury Tales* comprises twenty-four tales, each told in a different English-speaking voice. Chaucer captured English, the language of ordinary people, and displayed its great versatility and power.

It was not just mastery of English that made Chaucer's literary effort so superior. In *The Canterbury Tales*, Chaucer created characters from a cross-section of English society, from the gentry to the clergy to the servant class. These characters' clothes, their complexions, their styles of speaking, their values and beliefs, are all reflections of real people.

The Wife of Bath, for example, is a robust, ruddy-faced woman who sits easily upon her horse and tells of love and lust and marriage—she has had five husbands, so she knows what she is talking about.

The Pardoner is a corrupt character. (Medieval Pardoners were traveling preachers who collected payments in return for indulgences offered by the Roman Catholic Church. Indulgences were written guarantees that the payer would not suffer eternal punishment for sins.) Chaucer's Pardoner is an odd-looking, boylike man, vicious and selfish, who gives a fearsome sermon about gluttony, greed, and murder. Among Chaucer's other pilgrims are a merchant, a physician, a cook, a clerk, a nun, a monk, a friar, a squire, and a sergeant at law.

Chaucer lets his characters reveal themselves through their tales. At the same time, he reveals his own wonderful sense of irony and humor. Before the Miller begins his obscene tale, for example, Chaucer disavows any responsibility for it: ". . . putte me out of blame" is how he states it. He, as the writer, is there only to get the story down the way it was told to him; he jokingly warns the reader that there's some indecent material coming up that well-bred people may find offensive. His advice to such people: "Turne over the leef and chese another tale." (Turn over the leaf, or page, and choose another tale.) The advice must have been given with a wink. Who, then or now, would decide *not* to read a tale introduced with such a warning?

By the time Chaucer was writing *The Canterbury Tales*, he

was a mature poet who had already solved the problems posed by English speech rhythms. He used a syllable-and-stress pattern that he found especially suited to English— the five-beat line (still the most popular meter in English poetry). Here is how Chaucer described a young man, for example:

He wás as frésh as ís the month of Máy.

Chaucer wrote most of the tales using five-beat lines. He also ended every pair of lines with a rhyme, a form called rhyming couplets. Here is a sample—possibly the most famous lines of *The Canterbury Tales*, the opening of the prologue:

MIDDLE ENGLISH

Whan that Aprill with his shoures sote
The droghte of Marche hath perced to the rote
And bathed every veyne in swich licour
Of which vertu engendred is the flour . . .

MODERN NONRHYMED VERSION

When April with its sweet showers
has pierced the drought of March to the root,
and bathed every vein in such moisture
as has power to bring forth the flower . . .

The prologue goes on to describe the blossoming richness of spring, which stimulates people to take pilgrimages; thus Chaucer neatly sets up the frame for his story:

> *And specially, from every shires ende*
> *Of Engelonde, to Caunterbury they wende. . . .*
> *(And especially, from the ends of every shire*
> *in England, they come to Canterbury. . . .)*

Middle English is clearly much closer to today's English than it is to Old English. Yet today's readers of Chaucer often consult a translation, because there are some confusing differences between his language and our own.

First of all, spelling was far from standardized. Middle English writers simply picked a spelling that approximated the sounds of a word. The same word could be spelled differently by different writers, or even by the same writer in different places. There were no dictionaries to check; there was no such thing as correct spelling anyway.

Second, vocabulary has changed since the Middle English period. Some words, such as *vertu* (our *virtue*), have undergone meaning shifts. Chaucer's *vertu* meant "strength and power"; our *virtue* tends to describe goodness. Chaucer's *licour* is our *liquor*, but Chaucer's referred to liquid, not to alcohol. Many other Middle English words are no longer part of our vocabulary at all.

Third, the structure of Chaucer's sentences can challenge a modern reader. Even with modern spellings, the line "Of which virtue engendered is the flower" can be puzzling.

There is a fourth reason that Middle English can be difficult to understand. It is probably the most important reason, but it took a while for people to figure it out. In the centuries after Chaucer's death in 1400, his poetry was still known. But an odd thing had happened by the 1500's: The verses that Chaucer had fine-tuned to capture the natural rhythms of English now sounded awkward and halting, as if written by someone with a tin ear. Many of the couplets did not even rhyme! Seventeenth-century critics admired Chaucer for telling a good story—too bad, they said, the poor man was not skilled in writing verse.

Then, in the eighteenth century, scholars reasoned out what had happened. Sometime after Chaucer's death, the pronunciation of English had undergone major changes. Lines of poetry that had once had pleasing rhythms and delightful end rhymes now had neither. Chaucer's verse had lost those qualities because the sounds of Middle English words had changed.

Chaucer's words often had stresses different from later English versions. The Canterbury characters, for example, went on a pilgrimage. We say *PIL-grih-mij*; they said *pil-grih-MAH-juh*. Modern English has many words, like *pilgrimage*, with a final *e* that we do not pronounce. Chaucer would have given most of those *e*'s an unaccented vowel sound. When he spoke of his *tales* of Canterbury, he probably called them *TAH-lez*.

Chaucer also would have pronounced certain consonant sounds that we no longer hear: the flapped or trilled *r*, for

55

example, or the *l* in *folk*. Middle English speakers still used a Germanic *h* sound, spelled *gh* as in *droghte* (our modern *drought*), which they pronounced DRAWKH-*tuh* and we pronounce *drout*.

The most significant changes in pronunciation happened to Middle English vowel sounds. Chaucer was able to rhyme *liquor* and *flower* because they sounded like *lih-*KOOR and *floor*. But then came changes in the way that the long vowels of Middle English were pronounced. Language scholars call these changes the Great Vowel Shift, and it meant that many words underwent dramatic shifts in pronunciation. It was as if you stopped saying *who* and started pronouncing it *how* (although not so abruptly).

The Middle English word *maken*, for example, had the *a* vowel sound as in the modern word *father*. Speakers began to form the vowel sound differently in the mouth, and the word became *make*.

In Middle English, the word *teeth* was pronounced *tayth*. The vowel shifted to give *teeth* its present pronunciation.

The Middle English word *lyf* would have rhymed with the modern word *beef*. The vowel shifted to give the word the form it has today: *life*.

The word *good* in Middle English would have rhymed with the modern *rode*; the word *go* would have rhymed with our *raw*. The word *hous* was pronounced to rhyme with *moose* before it became our modern *house*.

Those are just a few examples. No wonder Chaucer's later readers were perplexed by his rhymes!

56

Books and Scholars

Just as language researchers rely on surviving Old English manuscripts to learn about the features of that lost language, they look to written works from the Middle Ages for clues about Middle English. Copies of Chaucer's manuscripts are an invaluable source of information. There are other sources as well, preserved through the centuries. Many have been preserved because of an invention that changed history, and changed the history of language too. The invention was the printing press.

When Chaucer had the opportunity and the money, he bought books. Books were rare, expensive items in medieval times. No two were exactly alike. All were copied by hand, some with stunning hand-painted drawings known as illuminations. Only the wealthy could afford shelves full of books. Everyone else had to save for an occasional purchase, or borrow one, or copy it, or translate it, or listen to someone read it aloud. Chaucer, by the end of his life, had amassed quite a collection, by medieval standards at least: a grand library of sixty books. Books were meant to be read, reread, reread again, and passed on to one's heirs. They were items of great beauty and value. In some medieval collections, the volumes were even chained to the shelf.

All that was about to change. About 1450, Johann Gutenberg, a German, introduced movable type to Europe. The printing of books began. Twenty-six years later, an entrepreneur named William Caxton established the first printing press in England. Type was set up, and perfect copies of the same page were lifted off the press. Suddenly all sorts of works could be printed in quantity.

Caxton translated and printed works for a public that was growing more and more literate. As books became more available in English, more people looked on reading and writing as useful and necessary skills. (After all, what great need had there been to read and write when books belonged only to the scholarly, who could read them in Latin? Or to the wealthy, who had the means to buy the few that were for sale?) Caxton's publications included religious works and popular works like Chaucer's tales and the legends of King Arthur.

Caxton chose to publish in English because that was the language people spoke and could learn to read, and because he would have no competitors in the European publishing world. The question that troubled him, however, was What *was* English exactly? Like Chaucer, Caxton was aware of the great diversity of the English tongue. He knew there were misunderstandings and confusion among English speakers. So many different dialects, or varieties of the language, were spoken in England, it was difficult to know what words to write. Not only did pronunciations vary from region to region, but the names for things also differed. Caxton told about a traveler who stopped at an inn and asked for eggs: *Egges* was what he said. The cook thought he was speaking French! Only when a fellow traveler asked for *eyren* were eggs willingly served up. What was the word to print, Caxton wondered, *egges* or *eyren*?

Caxton had witnessed language changes in his own lifetime. He wrote in the introduction to a book in 1490:

And certaynly our langage now used varyeth ferre [varies far] from that whiche was used and spoken whan I was borne.

He attributed this rapid variation to the influences of the stars, which caused the changeable nature of the English people. He was mistaken. The variation was the result of influences not from the heavens, but from the language changes that had been working their way into English ever since Anglo-Saxon times. The people of different regions had made different changes, and a confusing range of dialects was the result.

Caxton decided to write using the English dialect that was spoken around London. His decision made sense, since the London area was the center of government, trade, and learning. His decision was to have tremendous effects. Because his books were to spread over the country, the English printed in them was to become the standard. The dialect of London came to serve as the model for the English that is spoken and written today.

Although spelling would remain disorderly for more than a hundred years, Caxton tried to spell words more or less as they sounded. He also relied on general spelling patterns that had settled into Middle English writings. But vowel sounds were undergoing the Great Vowel Shift in Caxton's day, and Caxton's spellings did not capture those shifts. So it was that earlier speech forms became locked in place on the printed page, where confused spellers still find them today. (Just look at the seven different spellings for the one vowel sound we hear in these words: *moon*, *who*, *plume*, *rue*, *blew*, *soup*, *fruit*. To Middle English speakers, such different letter combinations made sense, since the vowel sounds heard in these words were not all alike.)

Printing also made a difference in the way people thought about the functions of the English language. For hundreds of years, English had been mainly an oral language. Suddenly it became a written one, and the nature of English communication was changed forever.

Writers mined the richness of English vocabulary. They experimented with synonyms (words with similar meanings). They discovered that ideas could be stated with varying degrees of simplicity or elegance, depending on which synonym was used. A word could come from English, the language of the common folk (a word such as *weak*, for example); or it could come from French, the language of literature (*frail*); or it could come from Latin, the language of scholarship (*fragile*). To this day, careful writers choose which of three categories of English synonyms fits their meaning best. Here are more examples:

English	*French*	*Latin*
rise	mount	ascend
fear	terror	trepidation
win	succeed	triumph
kingly	royal	regal

English	French	Latin
womanly	female	feminine
manly	male	masculine
ask	question	interrogate
holy	sacred	consecrated
fast	firm	secure

According to language historians, the Middle English period ended about 1500. Some place the end precisely at the year 1476, when the printing press was poised to leave its mark, so to speak. With the end of Middle English came the language period called Early Modern English, which lasted until 1650. In this modern period, the English language was filled with energy, spirit, and experimentation, just as were English arts, literature, and learning.

A reawakening of interest in the arts and sciences of ancient Greece and Rome had been taking place in continental Europe. This glorious revival of classical learning was known as the Renaissance (from a French word meaning "rebirth"). When the Renaissance emerged in England, new ideas burst forth. Printed books were spreading those ideas; education and literacy were spreading too. People were reading translations of the works of the ancient historians Thucydides and Herodotus, the philosopher Plato, the poets Homer and Virgil, and many other writers of the past. English writers, aroused by national pride and by the flexibility and power of their language, announced that English had lost its second-class status. It was a language that could say anything—and say it as beautifully as French or as profoundly as Latin. As one English writer of the time put it, "the English tung cannot prove fairer then it is at this daie. . . ."

But other sixteenth-century scholars were finding that English couldn't *exactly* say everything they wanted it to. English, it seemed, just didn't have enough of the right words. When English Renaissance writers began to translate the great Greek and Latin classics, they needed to express ideas for which English words did not exist. These translators probably could have come up with English equivalents if they had thought hard enough. They might have been able to think of phrases like "the will of the folk" or "common-rule," for example, but they found it quicker and easier to borrow a non-English term instead—in this case, *democracy* (from the Greek *demos*, "common people," and *-kratia*, "power").

Those scholars added a Greek or Latin word to a sentence here or a phrase there. Soon they were adding words at a furious rate. By the year 1600, ten thousand new words had entered English from the scholarly languages of the past, mostly from Latin. About half of those words have lasted until the present day. Consider the underlined words in the sentences below. Each of them was imported during the revival of classical learning in England:

A thermometer is an exact and ingenious instrument appropriate for use in the atmosphere.
If we create a crisis, a catastrophe may soon exist.
Let's celebrate with enthusiasm this athlete's superiority.
An encyclopedia that explains gives you confidence in your intelligence.

Not everyone thought that this surge of new words was a good thing. Sixteenth-century critics blamed the scholars for clouding English with "strange termes," and called the learned men "foolelosophers." Why, they asked, make up a new and fancy word when a perfectly good English expression will do? Suppose, for example, a writer needed a verb that meant "to briefly explain written material by arranging it under headings." The verb phrase *sum up* would have worked. But perhaps that didn't sound important enough. The scholars created a Greek-based word instead—*anacephalize* (*ana-*, "up"; *cephal*, "head"; *-ize*, "to make"). The word *anacephalize* did not last in English, by the way. But its equally long Latin-based counterpart did: *recapitulate* (*re-*, "again"; *capitulare*, "to put under headings").

Today critics still object to writing that requires the reader to wade through sentences clogged with Latinate words. To see why, compare these two sentences:

1. Obfuscatory lucubration is of nugatory efficacy.
2. Muddy writing cannot be understood.

Although the sentences have nearly identical meanings, the second one is obviously clearer. It is made only of words that come from Old English; the first sentence is made mostly of words originating in Latin. These sentences illustrate extreme positions. In reality writers do not limit themselves to Latin-based words. And it is not possible to write or speak on any subject for long using only words from England's Anglo-Saxon past.

English can be a subtle and expressive language because of the range and depth of its vocabulary, which comes from so many sources. It is a vocabulary that is, you might say, *enormous* (from Latin), *colossal* (from Greek), *huge* (from Old French), and *great* (from Old English).

So many Latin words are now firmly rooted in English that we would not be able to do without them. Critics past and present have made a useful point, however: Latin-based words often have a scholarly tone, and if they are overused, sentences may sound stilted and pretentious. Perhaps because Latin has long served as a language of the learned, it is the Latin-based words that tend to show up on vocabulary tests in school. The study of such words need not be a chore, though. It can be more like solving a puzzle, a fascinating puzzle made of word parts.

The English language has always built new words by adding meaningful parts before and after word roots. These add-ons are called prefixes and suffixes (*pre-* + *fix*, "to attach before"; *sub-* + *fix*, "to attach beneath"). Together they are known as affixes. Old English used the prefixes *for-*, *to-*, and *with-*, for example. Though we do not create new words with them anymore, they show up in such established words as *forget*, *today*, and *withstand*. The Old English word spelled *freondscipe* is what we call *friendship*; Old English *-scipe* suffix has been passed down as *-ship*. The suffix is still used in modern English to make words like *leadership* and *relation-ship*.

Other Old English suffixes have continued to be used widely. The suffix spelled *-lic* in Old English appears today as *-ly* whenever adverbs are needed: *slowly, quickly, coldly, warmly.* The Old English suffixes *-ness, -less,* and *-ful* still have end*less* use*fulness.* During the Middle English period, when French words were being rapidly made into English ones, French prefixes such as *dis-* and *en-,* and French suffixes such as *-ment, -able,* and *-ous,* were also borrowed. French affixes make it possible for us to say a sentence like this one: "We had an en*joyable* and harmon*ious* meeting because there were no *disagreements.*"

When Renaissance writers began to incorporate Latin words into English, a full supply of Latin prefixes and suffixes became available for word building.

Consider the Latin word *venire,* "to come." The root, often spelled *ven* or *vent* in English, shows up in the word *event* ("a result of something that *comes* or happens") and *invent* ("to *come* upon something"). When suffixes are added, even more words are built: *eventful, eventual, eventually, inventor, invention, inventive, inventively, inventory.*

Suffixes, along with the Latin prefix *ad-,* which means "toward" or "to," provide *adventure* and *adventurous.*

The Latin prefix *con-* means "together"; *convene* means "come together." Affix-adding creates *convenient, inconvenient, inconveniently, convenience,* and *inconvenience.* At a *convention* (where people *come* together), they reach agreement about *conventional,* or approved, behaviors. With affixes, we also get *conventionally, unconventional,* and even *unconventionality,* which means "the quality of not being conventional, or not following custom."

The Latin prefix *circum-* means "around." If you avoid a

65

problem by going around it, you *circumvent* it. You use *circumvention*.

The Latin prefix *inter-* means "between." Something that *intervenes* comes between two objects or events; an *intervention* is an act of coming between.

The Latin prefix *pre-* means "before." It shows up in the word *prevent*, which used to mean "come before" (as in the sentence "He prevents me by a week," which meant that he arrived a week before me). *Prevent* gradually changed to its present meaning: "to keep an event from happening by doing something beforehand." Adding affixes, we get *prevention*, *preventive*, *preventable*, *unpreventable*, and *unpreventability*.

With Latin roots and a multitude of available affixes, English words have grown in length, and English vocabulary has grown in size.

The Latin verb *struere* means "to arrange in piles, to build up." One form of that word—*structus*—appears as one of the building blocks in a tall pile of English words. The words *structure*, *substructure*, *superstructure*, *structural*, *construct*, *construction*, *constructive*, *constructively*, *reconstruct*, *reconstruction*, and *reconstructionist* are all clearly related to the original meaning of the Latin root. They all refer to the building of something.

If you do the opposite of building, however, you are *destructive*. You can cause *destruction* to something if it is *destructible* and not *indestructible*. With the growth of technology, it has also become possible to refer to something that can *self-destruct*. (By the way, why is it that English speakers never use *destruct* by itself, in a sentence such as "I'll *destruct* you if it's the last thing I do"? Why do we use the word *destroy* instead? The answer is that the word *destruct* was indeed introduced along with all the other Latin-based *struct* words. But it did not last. The word *destroy* had already entered English from an earlier Latin-based source, French, and that word was the one that stayed.)

When you build knowledge into learners, you *instruct* them. Added affixes give English *instructor*, *instruction*, *instructive*, and *instructively*.

The Latin prefix *ob-* means "against" in such words as *obstruct* ("to block or pile up against") and the affixed forms *obstruction*, *obstructive*, *obstructionist*, and *obstructionism*.

A related root, spelled *stru* in English, appears in *instrument* ("something that serves to build or furnish") and its built-up forms: *instrumental* and *instrumentation*.

The preceding paragraphs show that one Latin word meaning "to build" has directly furnished twenty-nine English words. And the list is not even complete. Among the words left out are the name of a movement in art known as *constructivism* and the legal term *constructionism*.

Many Latin roots have taken hold in English. They are now parts of English words that can be made long, longer, and longest by the addition of affixes. Three common roots are shown below. Because words change over time, it is not always easy to see the relationships between the meanings of a modern English word and its Latin root. If you find a few such puzzling words in the three lists below, a good dictionary should explain the connections.

-dict- (from the Latin *dicere*, "to say"; and *dictum*, "a saying"): *diction, dictionary, dictate, dictation, dictator, dictatorial, dictatorship, addict, addiction, benediction, malediction, contradict, contradiction, contradictory, dictum, edict, interdict, interdiction, predict, prediction, predictive, predictable, unpredictable, unpredictability*

-pend- (from the Latin *pendere*, "to be hanging," "to weigh," "to pay"): *pendulum, pendulous, perpendicular, pendant, pendent, append, appendage, appendix, suspend, suspense, suspension, pensive, depend, independent, compensate, compensation, spend, expense, expensive, expend, expenditure*

-scrib- and *-script-* (from the Latin *scribere*, "to write"; and *scriptus*, "written"): *script, Scripture, scribe, inscribe, inscription, ascribe, circumscribe, circumscription, conscript, conscription, proscribe, proscription, prescribe, prescription, subscribe, subscription, transcribe, transcript, transcription, describe, description, descriptive, indescribable, manuscript, postscript*

As English writers adopted words by the thousands by building upon Latin roots, English built up its vocabulary at an astounding rate. Sometimes the Latin-based word replaced a perfectly good English one, which is why we now say "Please don't *contradict* me," rather than "Please don't *withsay* me." At other times, the Latinate word filled a need for a term that did not exist in English: *Dictionary* is one example. More often, the new high-sounding word took its place beside a Middle English word and offered a more scholarly sounding synonym. Why describe a mule as merely *stubborn*, for example, when you can call it *intractable*, *inflexible*, *obdurate*, and *recalcitrant*?

The Latin word *manus* means "hand." Even though English has held on to its own perfectly good word *hand*, it has also grasped the Latin root *(man)* and created interesting side-by-side examples. English contributed the word *handbook*, for example; the Latin-based name for the same thing is *manual. Handcuffs* may be called *manacles. Handwriting* is sometimes called *manuscript. Handiwork* or *handicraft* can have meanings similar to *maneuver* and *manufacture.* The word *handiness* is used to describe skill at *manipulation.* The verb *to handle* means *to manage.* And the noun *handle* has a Latin counterpart too, although it is used only by those studying anatomy: The handle-shaped part of the hammer bone in the ear is known as the *manubrium.* Even *handkerchief* has a Latin partner: *maniple* is the name for a silk band that hangs near the wrist on certain clergymen's robes. In contrast to these partners, the word *hand-care* has been lost, outlived by *manicure.*

Although Latin was the major source of new words during the revival of learning in England, many other languages were contributing words as well. Greek, the other major classical language of scholarship, was also a source. Greek made many indirect contributions to English through Latin, since Latin words were often based on Greek ones. Educated writers also borrowed directly from Greek, which is why we have words such as *catastrophe* and *thermometer.* Because Greek is often the language of choice for scientists needing new terms, Greek-based word parts have long been combined to create words in science and technology, such as *telescope* ("distant watcher") and *microscope* ("small watcher"). The word parts listed below are just a small sampling of Greek offerings.

Greek Combining Forms

graph, graphy (*graphein*, "to write")	*auto* (*autos*, "self")
bio (*bios*, "life")	*logy* (*logos*, "word," "speech")
geo (*geo*, "earth")	*phone, phono* (*phone*, "sound")
tele (*tele*, "at a distance")	*photo* (*phos*, "light")

Just by combining the parts listed, we get *photograph, photography, autograph, geography, biography, autobiography, graphology, biology, geology, phonology, telephone, telephoto, telegraph,* and *phonograph.* And many more words are made with these and other Greek combining forms. You can sometimes look at spelling to tell that a word is originally Greek. The letters *ph* together standing for an *f* sound, or *ch* standing for a *k* sound, for example, are clues to an *archaic* ("ancient") source of interest to a budding **phi**lologist ("student of language").

Passage to Modern Times

Scholarly writers were not the only ones adding words to the English vocabulary of the sixteenth and seventeenth centuries. The great age of exploration had begun at the end of the fifteenth century. Adventurous navigators representing Spain, Portugal, the Netherlands, France, and England competed in the race for new trading routes, wealth, and lands. As a result of their discoveries, travelers and traders were returning regularly to Europe from Africa, Asia, and the continents of the western hemisphere known as the New World. They brought to England foreign foods and fashions, exotic plants and animals, exciting ideas, and—of course—new words.

From the Far East, for example, sailors brought back a pickled fish sauce with a name that sounded like *ke-tsiap*. Soon the name was being spelled *ketchup* or *catsup*. (Tomato ketchup—the variety of the sauce familiar today—came later.)

The islands of the Caribbean were known as the West Indies (it was while sailing west to reach the East Indies that Columbus found them). Spanish-speaking explorers of the West Indies picked up certain words from the native speakers, and it was not long before those words entered English: *barbecue*, *canoe*, *cannibal*, *hammock*, *hurricane*. Certain African words also traveled, by way of Spanish and Portuguese, into English: *corral*, *yam*, and *banana*, for example. Spanish speakers also gave English *apricot* (from an Arabic word) and *mosquito*.

A number of military terms were introduced from Italy, often indirectly through French or Spanish: *battalion*, *brigade*, *infantry*, *armada*, and *barricade*. Italy was a leading cultural center during the Renaissance, and English tourists considered

71

Italy the place to visit. They observed the clothing, the architecture, the arts, and the customs of the Italians, and they brought those influences back to England. Words of Italian origin thus became English ones: among them, *violin*, *trill*, *stanza*, *balcony*, *design*, and *granite*.

French also continued to make contributions to English, continuing a pattern begun centuries before.

The English language of this period was like a rapidly learning and growing child—playful, bright, energetic, and even wild and unruly at times. In the midst of this spirited language period, there arose an English writer with miraculous talents. His vocabulary was broader than any other writer's. He borrowed words, and he invented them. He played with words mischievously. And he controlled them like a master magician. He was a poet. But he was mainly a man of the theater—an actor and a playwright. His name was William Shakespeare.

Shakespeare lived from 1564 to 1616. Four centuries have passed since he wrote tragedies such as *Romeo and Juliet* and *Hamlet*, comedies such as *Twelfth Night* and *The Taming of the Shrew*, and history plays such as *Richard II* and *Henry V*. He wrote thirty-seven plays for the London theater companies he was a part of. All the plays continue to be read and performed today. Many have been made into modern musicals and movies. Shakespearean theater companies are still thriving. On Shakespeare's birthday, April 23, worshipful admirers gather to commemorate the contributions of this man, perhaps the greatest writer the English language has ever known.

Thousands upon thousands of pages of literary criticism have been written (and continue to be written) about Shakespeare's work.

Although he was a popular and successful playwright and poet in his own lifetime, Shakespeare probably would be struck speechless if he were to learn of all the attention given him in the past four centuries. When he wrote his plays, he considered his actors and his audiences, but not posterity. He never even bothered to supervise the publishing of his plays. After his death, two actors from his company gathered together the scripts and had them printed.

Shakespeare's work is known all over the world, often in translations. The translators who have attempted to change Shakespeare's English into Japanese, Russian, or any other language have faced a formidable task indeed. It is not that Shakespeare's ideas and plots and the emotions of his characters can't be expressed in other languages; it is that the power of Shakespeare's plays lies in his use of language. And Shakespeare's language is English.

The English that Shakespeare wrote was meant to be spoken aloud by actors on a stage. Shakespeare's success at linking meaning with sound may be one reason so many of his characters' lines are familiar expressions today. Even if you have never read a word by Shakespeare, you may still recognize some of the examples below.

Lord, what fools these mortals be!

All's well that ends well.

What's mine is yours, and what is yours is mine.

If music be the food of love, play on.

Some are born great, some achieve greatness,
and some have greatness thrust upon them.

The better part of valor is discretion.

A horse! a horse! my kingdom for a horse!

But, soft! what light through yonder window breaks?

O Romeo, Romeo! Wherefore art thou Romeo?

What's in a name? That which we call a rose
By any other name would smell as sweet.

Parting is such sweet sorrow.

Out, damned spot! out, I say!

Frailty, thy name is woman!

Neither a borrower, nor a lender be.

To be, or not to be: that is the question.

Friends, Romans, countrymen, lend me your ears.

Brevity is the soul of wit.

Every time you "have seen better days," have had "too much of a good thing," see something "in the mind's eye," or will "not budge an inch," you are using expressions introduced by Shakespeare. Did something happen "in the twinkling of an eye" or "melt into thin air?" Did you ever "laugh yourself into stitches" all "the live-long day"? Is it possible to be so "full of the milk of human kindness" that you "wear your heart upon your sleeve" and "love not wisely but too well"? Or must you be "cruel, only to be kind"? Can friends who are "poor but honest" ever hope to send "sweets to the sweet"? Well, "as good luck would have it," perhaps you think "there's time enough for that." But some of that is sure to be "neither here nor there." Are you beginning to get "my drift"? These quotations all come from Shakespeare. They are well-worn now, but once they were fresh and new — and appealing enough to travel down through the centuries to become clichés.

Also surviving four hundred years of travel are words that made their first written appearance in Shakespeare's works: *lonely*, *bump*, *assassination*, *submerged*, and *obscene*.

Because a living language never stands still, many of Shakespeare's usages have been left behind. The force and the beauty of his words and sentences are still appreciated by today's English speakers, but Shakespearean language is not exactly the same language we use today.

The reshaping of grammar that had begun back in the days of the Anglo-Saxons and Anglo-Danes was a long process. It was still going on in Shakespeare's time. (It is actually still going on today.) One difference was in the larger number of verb forms in Shakespeare's day. Shakespeare could have his characters say, for example, "thou shouldst" or "thou

75

sayest," or he could have them say (as we do) "you should" or "you say." A Shakespearean character could say "he heareth," or could use the modern -*s* ending and say "he hears." Shakespeare's English also included more pronouns. He, like us, could write *you*, *yourself*, *your*, and *yours*. Those are the only second-person pronouns most of us use today, but Shakespeare also used *thou*, *thee*, *thy*, *thine*, and *ye*. His characters could say not only "get you gone," but also "get thee gone."

Shakespearean speeches are filled with contractions such as *e'er*, *'tis*, *o'er*, *'tween*, *'gainst*, and *'twixt*. Such words sound old-fashioned (what dictionaries call Archaic) to us today, since contractions as a poetic device are now extremely rare. Other forms that Shakespeare used frequently are similarly archaic: the verbs *doth*, *hath*, and *hast*, for example. In addition to words that have been lost over the years, many of Shakespeare's words no longer have the same meanings. Because of these changes, today's readers of Shakespeare often rely on footnotes to help them with vocabulary.

Shakespeare's language was different in other ways. In his plays, Shakespeare referred to a daughter as "more braver"; to honor as "more sharper than your swords"; and to a stab from the knife of a disloyal friend as "the most unkindest cut of all." Today we have firmer rules about the use of such comparative forms. Shakespeare was able to use *honester*, *more larger*, and *less happier*; but we say *more honest*, *larger*, and *less happy*.

Modern speakers also have rules about the uses of negatives

such as *no*, *nor*, and *not.* It is considered nonstandard to say, for example, "I don't have nothing." (We think that means "I have something.") But Shakespeare was free to pile up as many negatives as he wanted, to emphasize those negatives, as in this sentence: "It is not, nor it cannot come to good."

Shakespearean sentences may also be built differently from modern sentences. The examples below will help you compare typical Shakespearean sentence structures with their modern English counterparts.

Shakespeare	*Modern Speakers*
Then saw you not his face.	So you didn't see his face.
The music likes you not.	You do not like the music.
Mistake me not.	Do not mistake me.
Work not so hard.	Do not work so hard.
They are come.	They have come.
Lies he not bed-rid?	Isn't he bedridden?
My master knows not but I am gone hence.	My master doesn't know that I haven't gone from here.
At this hour lies at my mercy all mine enemies.	At this hour all my enemies lie at my mercy.

Sentence structure and vocabulary have changed since Shakespeare's time. There have also been changes in pronunciation, which are harder to track down. What did Shakespeare's English sound like? Though no one can answer that question precisely, we do know that the English of 1600 would have been much more understandable to us than the Middle English of Chaucer's time. Most of the major pronunciation shifts had already occurred by 1600. But some were yet to occur. Shakespeare's actors and audiences would have pronounced *blood* to rhyme not only with *flood* but also with *mood* and *good*, for example. Lost rhymes are often clues to a past pronunciation. Consider the lines below:

> *Give sorrow words: the grief that does not speak*
> *Whispers the o'er-fraught heart, and bids it break.*

In Shakespeare's time, speakers did not pronounce *see* and *sea* alike. Words with the *ea* spelling probably were pronounced with the vowel sound that remains today only in *break, steak,* and *great.* The words at the ends of the lines above, *speak* and *break,* would have rhymed.

The lines above are worth looking at for more than their end rhymes. They come from the tragedy *Macbeth* and are words of consolation and advice to a character who has been dumbstruck on learning that his entire family has been slaughtered by his enemy. Simply stated, the advice is this: Speak about your sorrow; if you keep your grief inside, you will suffer more pain. But Shakespeare knew better than to state the advice so matter-of-factly. As a poet and a dramatist, he understood the role that language plays in making an audience feel the unbearable tension of that moment, share the man's sorrow, and weep for him. So Shakespeare writes about the power of grief: It can speak aloud, or it can whisper; but when it whispers, it tells the "o'er-fraught" (burdened) heart to break.

Grief, of course, cannot literally speak or whisper—Shakespeare is using a figure of speech called personification. In personification, human and living qualities are given to something that is not alive. A related figure of speech is called a metaphor. Poets use metaphors to make comparisons in which one thing is said to be another. Shakespeare's character Romeo uses metaphors as he looks up at Juliet at her window:

> *But, soft! what light through yonder window breaks?*
> *It is the east, and Juliet is the sun.*

Poets use metaphors to paint images and provoke surges of emotion and understanding. The successful use of figurative language, such as personification and metaphor, is one reason Shakespeare's lines are so memorable.

Shakespeare showed what the English language could become in the hands of a master poet. But in any age, how many people are master poets? Shakespeare had unique talents. The people who lived in his time used the English language for much less elegant purposes: simply to describe, relate, and explain. Here is an example of prose from the same period (original spellings are preserved):

> . . . From this place we sailed round about this headland, almost all the points of the compass, the shore very bold; but as no coast is free from dangers, so I am persuaded, this is as free as any; the land somewhat lowe, full of goodly woods, but in some places plaine. . . .

. . . Comming ashore, we stood a while like men ravished at the beautie and delicacie of this sweet soile. For besides divers cleere lakes of fresh water (whereof we saw no end), Medowes very large and full of greene grasse; even the most wooddy places (I speake onely of such as I saw) doe grow so distinct and apart, one tree from another, upon greene, grassie ground somewhat higher than the plaines, as if Nature would shew herselfe above her power artificiall.

These paragraphs come from an account of a voyage taken in 1602. The traveler describes landing in an area that he calls the north part of Virginia. Today we know it as the New England area of Cape Cod. New England would soon be settled by English-speaking people seeking religious freedom and new economic opportunities. By the middle of the seventeenth century, England's language would be heard elsewhere in other New World settings: in Virginia, Maryland, Nova Scotia, Newfoundland, Honduras; on the islands of Bermuda, Barbados, Jamaica, Antigua. English had entered its modern age.

During the eighteenth and nineteenth centuries, England would go on to expand its trade and shipping industries and establish settlements all over the world. It would spread its influences to other North American colonies, including Canada; to India, South Africa, Nigeria, Australia, New Zealand, Singapore, Hong Kong; and elsewhere in the Pacific, in Asia, in Africa, in South America.

In Shakespeare's time only about four million people lived in England (about the population of present-day Louisiana).

At its peak of influence in the nineteenth century, the British Empire had spread to one fourth the population of the world. In each new land, English was the language of the settlers and the governing officials. Over the years it took hold as the native language of some people and as the second language of others. Today English is the most widely spoken language on earth.

English speakers around the world are able to understand one another even though not all English is alike. Pronunciation differs among speakers of British English, American English, Australian English, Jamaican English, and other forms. Each group of English speakers uses certain words and expressions that the other groups do not use. Although these differences do not prevent communication, English speakers are sometimes puzzled by the language of other English speakers. Special reference books, similar to foreign-language dictionaries, help clear up trouble spots. A British-American dictionary, for example, explains that an American *apartment* is a British *flat*; to *line* up in the United States is to *queue* up (pronounced *kew*) in England; that a *billion* in the United States is *one thousand million* in England; and that an American car has a *hood*, *trunk*, and *windshield*, which are known in England as a *bonnet*, *boot*, and *windscreen*.

Why are there such differences? As new lands were settled, English speakers needed words for the strange animals and plants they were seeing, for the landforms they had never known in England, for the kinds of weather they had never experienced. English speakers at home and abroad continued to vary their pronunciations of words, to borrow words from other languages, to stop using some words, to change the meanings of others, and to create new words for new purposes.

Whether arriving in a new homeland or staying on its original island, the English language continued to do what it had always done—to change. Once English spread beyond the borders of its island home, its history turned into not just one story but many stories.

III

Root Relationships

If you go back far enough, to the Indo-European sources of so many modern and ancient languages, you will find an enormous number of words in modern English that share root relationships. But it is not necessary to look that far back to discover such relationships. You need only think about the stages discussed in the preceding chapters: Old English, Middle English, and the beginnings of Modern English; and the influences of Anglo-Saxons, Anglo-Danes, Anglo-Normans, and Renaissance scholars. The sounds, meanings, and spellings of modern words may be clues to a shared past. The easiest way to be a word detective and follow those clues is to open a good dictionary. You may find answers like those that follow.

A SHIRT OR A SKIRT?

Have you ever wondered why the words *skirt* and *shirt* look so much alike? A skirt and a shirt are different articles of clothing, after all. It is true that their meanings are now different, but the similarities in *skirt* and *shirt* are a clue to a past relationship. You may recall from Chapter I that speakers of Old Norse spoke the consonant combination *sk*, while Old English speakers used *sh* (which they spelled *sc*). The Old Norse word *skyrta* named a garment that covered the body from neck to knees. A similar garment was called *scyrte* in Old English. Over time, the names separated, just as the garment itself separated—*shirt* for the upper body, *skirt* for the lower.

A TAILOR MUST PAY ATTENTION TO DETAILS

Tailor and *details* are words cut from the same cloth, so to speak. Both come from an Old French word, *taillier*, "to cut or split." A tailor is someone who cuts. A detail is a piece cut away from the whole. Although they share a root relationship with each other, neither *tailor* nor *detail* is connected to the word for what a dog wags. That word *tail* comes from an Old English source. (Of course, just to confuse matters, there is a homograph—a word that is spelled the same—for *tail*. That *tail* is a legal term referring to the inheritance of an estate. Like *tailor* and *detail*, it comes from the Old French *taillier*.)

THE SECRETARY'S SECRET

The word *secretary* does indeed come from *secret*—a secretary's original purpose was to keep secrets. The word *secret* entered English from Latin by way of Old French. The Latin word *secretum* referred to a hidden place, where government officials could discuss affairs of state privately. Such a department is now often called a secretariat, and it is governed by a secretary. The title of *secretary* is no longer limited to government officials, such as the secretary of labor or the treasury; it refers to anyone who handles clerical affairs for an employer. Other related words include *secrecy* and *secretive*, and the biological term *secretion*, which names a substance, such as mucus, that is *secreted* ("separated out of") cells or the body.

A KERNEL OF CORN

"This kernel of corn did not pop." That sentence sounds fine. It may seem a little silly, however, if you think about the root relationship between *kernel* and *corn*. Old English speakers referred to cereal grains such as oat, wheat, and barley as *corn*. (What Americans call corn is a New World plant unknown in England when Old English was spoken.) An Old English *cyrnel* was a single grain or seed—a "little corn." Today when we speak of a kernel of corn, we ignore the root relationship. After all, we might feel foolish if we realized what we were saying: "This little corn of corn did not pop."

ALL ABOUT HORNS

Corn grows in the ground. A corn can also grow painfully on a foot. Are those two corns related? No. The paragraph before this one points out that *corn* (the name for the plant) comes from Old English. The *corn* that refers to the thickening of the skin arrived in English later, through Old French. That word *corn* shares some interesting root relationships.

Old English speakers—and modern English speakers too—

called each bony growth on an animal's head a *horn.* Meanwhile, Old French speakers, borrowing more directly from the Latin word *cornu*, called the thing a corne. When English speakers began to borrow from French, they used the word *corne* not to replace their own perfectly good *horn*, but to name any hard, thick growth that resembled the texture of an animal's horn. Another word similarly related to the Latin *cornu* is *cornea*, which names the thick, circular tissue that covers the lens of the eye.

Resemblance to the horn of an animal's head has led to other words with the *corne* root: *cornucopia* (a horn of plenty), *unicorn* (a one-horned animal of fable), *cornet* (an instrument blown like the horn of an animal), and even *corner* (a place where sides meet in a point).

The ancient Greeks also had a word for an animal's horn — *keras.* A number of English words share a relationship with that Greek root. Perhaps you've heard of 14- or 24-*karat* gold. A karat (also spelled *carat*) is a measure that tells how much pure gold is in a metal mixture. A carat is also a unit of weight for precious stones. Today it is equal to 200 milligrams. But in ancient times, a karat was the weight of four seed grains, each of which was shaped like a "little horn."

Another horn-shaped item probably shares the ancient Greek root too. It is a homophone (a word that sounds the same) for *carat* or *karat*. It is spelled *carrot*.

The Greek root *keras* sometimes appears in English spelled with a *c* instead of *k*. Consider these two animal names:

rhinoceros and *triceratops*. If you put together the Greek elements below, you should be able to translate each name.

rhino-: "nose"   *-cer-*: "horn"

-ops-: "face"   *tri-*: "three"

The Greek *keras* appears in another English word. It is the name for the protein that forms our fingernails and hair and also forms animals' hoofs and . . . horns. The word is *keratin*.

A MOUSE WITH MUSCLE

The Old English and Latin words for *mouse* were the same: *mus*. The Latin word for "little mouse," *musculus*, has been passed down to us as *muscle*. How is a muscle like a "little mouse"? It was the shape or the rippling movement of a muscle that suggested a little mouse under the flesh—or so it seemed to Latin speakers long ago.

A homophone for *muscle* is spelled *mussel*. A mussel is a kind of shellfish. Its name comes from the same Latin source. Its motions inside its shell resemble those of a muscle, which in turn resemble those of a "little mouse," *musculus*.

AN EXPLOSION OF APPLAUSE

When performers in ancient Rome wanted an audience to show appreciation, they would give the command *Plaudite!* "Clap your hands!" The Applause signs in today's television studios serve the same purpose. They also share the same root. The word *applaud* comes from the Latin *plaudere*, "to

beat or strike, especially with one hand against the other."
Ad- and *plaudere* combine to mean "to clap toward or at."
Hand clapping is not always warm and appreciative, however.
Loud claps can serve to startle and chase away. When the
prefix *ex-* is used with the Latin root, the meaning is quite
different. The Latin word *explodere* means "to drive out by
clapping." So it is that the modern English words *applaud*
and *explode* are both related to the clapping of hands.

CAN YOU DEMONSTRATE HOW YOU DID IT, DR. FRANKENSTEIN?

Ancient Romans believed that certain omens, or signs, showed
the will of the gods. The name for such a predictive sign
was *monstrum.* Soon that word came to refer to the supernatural
being that was signified by the omen—a word that has passed
into English as *monster.* Since an omen pointed out the gods'
wishes, another Latin form of the word meant "to point
out, to show, or to prove." That word has entered English
as *demonstrate.* Now it is possible to speak of a *monstrous
demonstration* or a *demonstrative monster.* Could the ancient Romans have predicted our use of such words?

IS GRAMMAR GLAMOROUS?

Today we use the word *grammar* to refer to certain features
of language—relationships among word parts, words, and
sentences. Modern students learn the rules of grammar, for
example, in English and foreign-language courses. And educated people try to avoid the misuse of words that is often
labeled "bad grammar." But in the Middle Ages, the word

grammar referred to the study of Latin in particular, and to learning in general. Many people tended to associate learning with the magic arts. That connection to magical, occult qualities showed up in the Scottish form of the word: *glammar* . . . or *glamor* (which came to mean "magic, enchantment, or spell"). That meaning has been replaced by the present meaning of *glamor*: "charm, excitement, and romance." Even though the root relationship between *grammar* and *glamor* is now overlooked, it is still possible to find glamor in grammar (just ask a linguist).

WHAT'S ALL THAT NOISE?

Suppose that you feel sick to your stomach. Should you say that you feel *nauseated* or that you feel *nauseous*? Either word makes the point, according to most speakers. Some writers argue, however, that the words have slightly different meanings—that you should say "I feel nauseated" when you have a queasy stomach and are suffering from nausea. Something that is nauseous, on the other hand, is so disgusting and repulsive that it causes you to feel nausea.

We owe our thanks to the ancient Greeks for all this nauseating talk, since they were the original users of the word. When they said *nausia*, they meant "seasickness." The modern English word *nausea* is thus related to a number of words having to do with the sea and sailing—for example, *nautical* ("having to do with ships, sailors, and navigation") and *astronaut* ("someone who sails, or navigates, among the stars"). Traveling through Latin, Greek nautical words changed their sounds to enter English as *naval*, *navy*, and *navigate* — all, of course, having to do with the sea.

The root traveled yet another route, through Old French, to land in English as a word that we no longer associate with ships, sailing, or seasickness. That word is *noise*. Noise? The meaning connection between *nausea* and *noise* may not be immediately apparent. But the same unpleasant confusion that takes place on a ship full of seasick sailors can take place elsewhere. That is why ancient speakers used the word for "seasickness" to name other loud, disorderly situations. And the word, no longer limited to its shipboard uses, made its way to modern English as *noise*.

TADPOLE OR POLLIWOG?

To gather information about people's opinions and habits, you might take a poll. The kind of survey called a poll is actually a head count, since *poll* has meant "head" since Middle English times. And Middle English speakers combined *tadde* ("toad") with *pol* ("head") to create the name for the frog or toad that has not reached its adult stage — the tadpole seems to be made of a tail attached to a "toad head." Other Middle English speakers took a look at the immature frog wiggling about in ponds and called the creature a *polwygle* ("head wiggle"). The name is now *polliwog*. Which name do speakers in your region prefer? To find out, take a poll.

HOSTILE GUESTS

Various forms of the Latin word *hospes*, which means both "host" and "guest or stranger" have entered English in different shapes. From words that originally referred to places of refuge, we now have such settings as *hostels* (shelters for young travelers), *hotels* (places that offer rooms and meals for travelers), *hospitals* (places that provide treatment for the sick), and *hospices* (originally shelters for the needy run by religious orders—now coming to mean shelters for the dying). We also speak of those who serve guests as *hosts* and *hostesses*, and of their welcoming behavior as *hospitality*.

Of course, a stranger was not always someone to be welcomed. Latin speakers used another form of the word, *hostis*, to mean "enemy." From that root, we have the *hostile* behavior of an enemy, or *hostility*.

Another word derived from the same Latin root meaning "guest" is *hostage*, although someone held for ransom is a guest of a most peculiar sort.

One Latin root is thus the source of a variety of hostile and hospitable terms. The name for those who are served—*guests*—however, comes from another source: Old Norse. That is why English, unlike Latin, makes a clear distinction between host and guest.

EXTRATERRESTRIAL TERRITORY

Mapmakers used to label unexplored regions *Terra Incognita*, Latin for "unknown land." We still use that term to refer to the unknown. Modern English speakers also use the Latin words *terra firma* to name the solid ground underfoot—"After a long sea voyage, it feels great to be on good old *terra firma* again." The Latin word *terra* means "land," and it appears as the root in a number of English words.

The word *terrace* used to refer to a pile of earth, such as a raised bank. *Terrace* still retains the meaning "platform," but today a terrace is often paved or tiled, rather than made of earth. It is easy to see the "earth" meaning in words such as *terrain* ("the features of a land region"), *territory* ("area of land"), *terrarium* ("a small earth-filled enclosure for plants and small animals"), *inter* and *interment* ("to bury" and "burial"), *subterranean* ("underground"), *mediterranean* ("middle of the land"—the Mediterranean Sea is almost completely surrounded by land), and *terrestrial* ("of the earth"). Extraterrestrials, the subject of so many science fiction movies, are creatures that are "outside of the earth."

The small busy dogs called terriers also owe their name to the Latin word for "earth." They used to be known as *chiens terriers*; the French word for "dog" is *chien*, and these "earth dogs" were adept at digging animals out of burrows. The *chien* part of the name was eventually dropped. The French also used the *terra* root in their word for an earthenware bowl. They called it a *terrine*. English speakers borrowed the word but changed the spelling. We ladle our soup from a *tureen*.

ELEVEN ONIONS

The Latin word *unus* has been the source of a number of English words that mean "one" and "oneness": *unit*, *united*, *unity*, *unify*, *unison*, and *unique*, for example, as well as words with the prefix *uni-* such as *unicycle*.

A Latin form of the word named both a state of oneness

and a plant with an edible bulb, whose layers formed a unified whole. Those two meanings have passed into English, although the words have taken slightly different forms: *union* and *onion*.

The Latin word meaning "one" came from an Indo-European root that had also branched off into the Germanic language that led to Old English. The Old English version of the root has led to the modern word *one* (the odd *w* pronunciation came much later—in Old English, the word sounded like *ahn*). Old English also used the "one" root to form *a*, *an*, *alone*, and *once*. And when Old English speakers wanted to count *one* past their ten fingers, they used the word *endleofan*, which meant "one left" (ten plus one left over). After some sound and spelling changes, the word became what we know today: ten plus one equals *eleven*.

YOUNG AND SURLY SENATORS?

According to the United States Constitution, members of the U.S. Senate must be at least thirty years old. That is not old at all. But in ancient Rome, the home of the first senate, senators were, by definition, old men. The Latin word root *sen* means "old." Other modern words that share this old root are *senior* ("elder"), *senile* ("aged, with mental and physical deterioration"), and—by way of the French *seigneur*—*sire* and *sir*, which are respectful names for a nobleman. Since a sir could be haughty, the word *sirly* came to mean "gruffly arrogant." Today that word has undergone a slight meaning and spelling change. Someone who is sullen and rude may be called *surly*. Surly behavior is not unknown in the Senate, though the root relationship between the words is now well hidden.

ABOUT AS LIVELY AS A VEGETABLE

Often, when we want to make fun of people's lack of energy or wit, we compare them to vegetables. The person who spends the day vaguely staring at the living-room television, for example, is a "couch potato," and anyone too inactive may be described as "just vegetating." These meanings are exactly the opposite of the meaning of the root from which *vegetable* grows. The Latin word *vegere* means "to enliven, or to make something come alive," and it is related not only to the name for a living, growing plant—*vegetable*—but also to another Latin word, *vigere*, which has given us such obviously alert and energetic words as *vigor*, *invigorate*, *vigil*, and *vigilant*.

TASTY PASTE

With the exception of a few kindergartners, most people do not eat paste. Right? Wrong. The Latin word *pasta*, meaning "paste," is the name for dough. The word passed into Italian, from which we have borrowed it as the general name for all such dough products: spaghetti, lasagna, macaroni, vermicelli (which, by the way, translates as "little worms"), and many more. All are pasta. And the paste that turns into cakes is called *pastry*.

CHUMS, COMRADES, AND PHOTOGRAPHY

One English word for a large room, *chamber*, comes from the Latin word *camera*. The name for someone who shared

96

a room (a *camera*) became *camarada* in Spanish, traveled into French as *camarade,* and then into modern English as *comrade.* English university students were also using the term *chamber fellow* to name a roommate, and this word shortened over time into *chum. Camera obscura* is the full Latin name for an early photographic device. The name means "dark chamber" and has since been shortened to the familiar *camera.*

RIVER RIVALS

The Latin word for a brook or stream is *rivus,* which is the source of the English word *river.* Latin speakers referred to those who lived on the riverbanks as *rivales*, a word that eventually entered English as *rivals.* Do you see the connection between those who dwell on the riverside and those who compete for a trophy or a lover? The connection is this: Because a river is often a natural boundary between families or between nations, those on opposite riverbanks are not always cooperative with one another. Sometimes they fight over the use of the river. In other words, people who live on the banks of the *river* may become *rivals.*

A LARGE FOOD BUDGET COULD MAKE ONE'S BELLY BULGE

Speakers of Old English used the word *bælig* (pronounced somewhat like BAL-*lee*) to name a pouch or bag made of animal skin. The word was related to the Latin *bulga,* which also named a leather bag. Over time, the Old English word changed so that it referred to the part of a living animal called the *belly.* Meanwhile, the Latin word *bulga* traveled another route to end up in Middle English as *bulge,* which

97

was the name for a pouch. It is not too hard to see how the image of a swollen pouch could suggest a new meaning for the word, and that is probably how the modern *bulge* ("a swelling") arrived. Yet another word has traveled into modern use from the Latin *bulga*. Middle English speakers called a wallet a *bouget*; today the word is *budget*.

GENERAL MEANINGS

Ladies and Gentlemen: One root that has engendered a generous supply of modern English words is the Latin word *genere*, "to give birth to" or "to produce or cause." Over the generations, people of both genders, from generals to engineers to geniuses, have used those words to talk about engines, generators, germs, and genetics. It may be unwise to generalize, but this Latin root has been the progenitor of an ingenious vocabulary.

In the section immediately above, there are sixteen English words with a root relationship. Can you find them all?

IV

Names Come to Life

The English language, as you have seen, has gone through some remarkable changes. Trying to track a language in motion can be a dizzying experience. Sometimes a closer look at certain categories of words can help you to pick out patterns. One such category is especially important: names of living things. Important, because what could have been more essential to our early word-using ancestors than the animals they hunted and the plants they gathered? These life forms made human life itself possible. Even when human beings were no longer just hunters and gatherers but had become explorers, tourists, colonists, and scientists, they continued to seek names for unfamiliar animals and plants.

If you saw a creature for the first time, how would you go about naming it? Perhaps you would use one of the patterns of labeling that people have followed throughout history. These naming strategies are built on human imagination, inventiveness, intelligence . . . and ignorance. Some of those strategies are described in this section, in stories behind the names for animals and plants.

Animal Names on the Move

How much wood would a woodchuck chuck
If a woodchuck could chuck wood?

That tongue twister is an old favorite. Its author must have noticed that something was odd—and humorous—about the name of this animal. A woodchuck most definitely does not "chuck wood." What's more, no one has a clear idea of what the animal would be doing if it *were* chucking wood. (Tossing sticks about, perhaps?) How did this North American mammal get its name?

When English-speaking settlers first came to America hundreds of years ago, they saw many plants and animals that were new and strange. It was common for settlers to ask the native people, "What is that called?" The answers varied and sometimes were misheard. The Cree Indians, for example, called the animal *otchek*. Algonquin and Ojibwa Indians used similar-sounding names: *otchok, otchig, wuchak, wejack*. The animal they were describing may actually have been a long and graceful marten or fisher, and not the chunky creature of tongue-twister fame. But the settlers heard the name and changed it into something that sounded more like words in English: *woodchuck*.

More confusion arose when different settlers called the animal by other names. In the United States, February 2 is Groundhog Day. On that day, according to popular legend, the groundhog comes out of its burrow and looks around.

If it sees its shadow, another six weeks of winter are on the way. February 2 could just as easily have been called Woodchuck Day, for the woodchuck and the groundhog are the same animal. So is the whistle-pig.

Because the animal resembled a European rodent known as a marmot, some settlers from Europe used the name *marmot*. The Lenape Indians used the name *monack*, based on a word in their language that meant "to dig." Settlers who heard the Lenape word also called the animal a monack, sometimes pronouncing it *moonack*.

The popular names for animals can vary greatly, even among speakers of the same language. The language of science, however, must be precise. Scientists who study animals must share the same terms, regardless of their own different languages and their own varied names for living things.

It is only natural that science, looking for an international language, has depended upon the same languages that served scholars throughout history: Latin and Greek. Scientists also look to the work of a man who lived more than two hundred years ago.

Carl von Linné (1707–1771) was a Swedish medical doctor and naturalist. He designed a practical system for classifying all known forms of life. His system of names relied on two basic units, *genus* (group) and *species* (kind). He wrote his works in Latin and used a Latinized version of his own name, Carolus Linnaeus (KAR-uh-lus lih-NEE-us), which is the name we know him by today.

Our knowledge about plants, animals, and other living organisms has changed enormously since Linnaeus' time. But we still use the Linnaean naming system. Despite the number of popular names it may have, every living thing has one two-part scientific name, given in Latin or Greek. The North American animal known as the woodchuck/groundhog/whistle-pig/marmot/monack, for example, is given the scientific name *Marmota monax*. The genus label, *Marmota*, is Latin for "mountain mouse" and is used for all marmots world-wide. The species label, *monax*, is a Latinized form of the Lenape word *monack*, and refers to the North American rodent specifically.

So you see, when the scientific name is used, the puzzling question *How much wood would* Marmota monax *chuck?* is a question that no longer needs to be asked.

One small North American rodent is a member of the same squirrel family to which the woodchuck belongs. When settlers pointed to the speedy little thing and asked the Indians, "What is that called?" the answer was *atchitamon*. In the language of the Ojibwa, the word meant "headfirst" and referred to a squirrel that scrambled headfirst down a tree. The settlers transformed the name *atchitamon* into *chitmunk*. And *chitmunk* sounds close to the version of the word we use today: *chipmunk*.

The process that led to the popular names *woodchuck* and *chipmunk* has been repeated with other animal names.

Take the mongoose — if you dare. This powerful, wiry

mammal is respected in its native India as a fearless killer of poisonous snakes. It does not look or act like a goose, so what is *goose* doing in its name?

India was once part of the British Empire. It became home to English-speaking settlers who heard the name *mangus* (from Marathi, one of the languages of India) and changed it into something more like English words. Thus, a mangus became a mongoose.

A tale is told of a British officer who had been stationed in colonial India. After returning to England, the officer found that his garden was overrun with rats and mice. He thought immediately of the capable snake and rodent killers he had seen in India, so he wrote to friends still there: "Please send me two mongeese."

"*Mongeese* can't be right," he said to himself, and tore up the letter. "Please send me two mongooses," he wrote on another sheet. But that, too, looked wrong.

His third version, however, brought a smile of satisfaction. "Please send me one mongoose," he had written. "And while you're at it, send me another."

Knowing that the animal's name has nothing to do with a goose or with geese, you would, of course, have had no problem identifying the correct plural: *mongooses*. Mongooses belong to the genus *Herpestes*, "snake pest."

Indri indri is the scientific name for a huge-eyed animal related to monkeys. The animal is native to Madagascar, a large island in the Indian Ocean. An eighteenth-century French naturalist was the first European to report on the creatures of Madagascar. The native people introduced this naturalist to the local wildlife. They pointed to an animal and announced, "Indry!" In their language, *indry* simply meant "Look!" But the naturalist dutifully noted that the animal was called an indri (IN-dree). This mislabeled creature is a member of the lemur (LEE-mer) family.

Another Madagascar lemur, also noted by the same visiting naturalist, is called an aye-aye. That was closer to the native name, which was probably based on the sound of the animal's cry—an unpleasant cross between a screech and a scrape.

Linnaeus was the first to apply the name *lemur* to both the indri and the aye-aye. The animals are most active at night. Their enormous eyes shine out of the darkness with a ghostly light. Linnaeus was reminded of the lemures (lem-YOOR-eez), the frightening spirits of the dead that the ancient Romans believed in.

Those who visit and settle new lands may change or borrow animal names from native speakers. As a result, our dictionaries now include such words as *chipmunk* and *aye-aye*. At other times, settlers and visitors do something a little different— they bring animal names with them. The odd name of a famous American bird is one result.

Benjamin Franklin, one of the greatest American thinkers and statesmen of the eighteenth century, knew an American bird when he saw one. Franklin was a member of the committee assigned to select the seal of the United States of America. He was against the choice of the bald eagle. He said that the bald eagle was "a bird of bad moral character." (Our national symbol is, in fact, not above stealing food from other birds and feeding on already dead prey.) Franklin preferred the turkey as a symbol of the new American nation. He believed that the turkey was "a much more respectable bird." He also argued that the turkey was "a true native of America."

The turkey is indeed a true native of North America. Wild turkeys were plentiful for the Indians and pioneers. Hunters relied on these numerous birds as a major source of food. No holiday is more American than Thanksgiving, and think of what Thanksgiving would be without turkeys. But if the turkey is so all-American, what is it doing with the name of a nation in the Near East?

English settlers in America were responsible. They gave the bird its name because it resembled a bird they had known back in England. That bird, the African guinea fowl, had been first brought to England by Turkish traders. Because the suppliers of the bird were from Turkey, the English came to call the bird a turkey fowl, a turkey hen, or a turkey cock. In time the name was shortened to *turkey*.

The turkey's name has continued its travels to the present day. Speakers have considered the bird's appearance, its behavior, its condition—and have formed several creative connections:

We walked out halfway through the second act of that play. What a *turkey*!

Did you hear about the guy who sent away for a genuine diamond ring that was advertised for only two dollars? What a *turkey*!

I'll never buy another E-Z-Mo lawn mower as long as I live. What a *turkey*!

A stage play that is especially boring or poorly performed has come to be known as a turkey. Any awkward or foolish person may receive today's slang label of *turkey*. And any worthless thing is a turkey too. It seems that the turkey is a victim not only on Thanksgiving, but all year round.

A history similar to *turkey* is behind the name of a common pet, the guinea pig. During the 1600's, the average English citizen had only a dim awareness of international geography. The English used the name *guinea* to refer to anything African, not just to what is now the west-central African nation of Guinea. At that time, slave ships regularly traveled from the African coast to the New World and back to England. Sailors on those ships brought back plants and animals from the New World. Sailors returning from the South American country of Brazil, for example, introduced a furry rodent to England. Because the animal was associated with sailors on African slave ships, it was described as a guinea pig. The pig label may have been applied because of the animal's shape and squealing voice. The guinea pig, as it turns out, is neither a Guinea native nor a pig.

"Do you want to be the first to taste my homemade pie?"
"No, thanks. I prefer not to be a *guinea pig.*"

Like many names for animals, *guinea pig* has taken on an extended, figurative meaning over time. Specially bred guinea pigs have been widely used as laboratory animals in scientific experiments. We often compare ourselves to guinea pigs when we feel at risk, as if we are the subjects of an experiment.

Have you ever heard a canary sing? Ever since the fifteenth century, when the French king Louis XI introduced canaries to Europe, the male birds have been bred to sing while caged. Its sweet song is what makes this bird so appealing as a pet. No one who has ever listened to this little yellow bird would think of comparing its tuneful song to the yelps and howls of a dog. But the name *canary* comes from the Latin word for dog, *canis.* Why?

The bird called a canary is native to a group of islands in the Atlantic Ocean, off the northwestern coast of Africa. The Romans referred to the largest of these islands as Canaria, because of the many dogs (in Latin, *canes*) found there. The Spanish, to whom the islands now belong, call the largest one Gran Canaria. In English the group is known as the Canary Islands, and it is home to the canary bird. Over time, the canary bird has become simply the canary.

In the early 1920's, the songwriter Harry Woods created a hit that remained popular for decades. When he came up with the opening line "When the red red robin comes bob bob bobbin' along," he must have known that people love to love the robin. Those fond feelings are the reason for this bird's name.

Throughout Europe the robin—with its cheerful song and lighthearted manner—was always regarded with affection. It was even considered bad luck to harm a robin. In England the bird was called a redbreast. It was a common practice to add a human nickname before the name of a well-known creature (the sparrow, for example, was known as Philip Sparrow), and the likable redbreast became Robin Redbreast. It was the added name—*Robin*—that stuck. *Redbreast* was gradually dropped, especially in the United States.

The story of the robin must be completed with one final point. The American bird called a robin is not the same as the bird the English call a robin. The European robin is smaller than the American one. The American bird is one of the first migrating birds to return north at the end of winter, which is why it is welcomed as a sign of spring. The European robin, on the other hand, might not leave home at all. The American robin is actually a red-breasted thrush. Scientists know how to avoid confusion, however. The scientific name *Turdus migratorius* ("traveling thrush") tells scientists exactly which bird it is that comes bob bob bobbin' along each spring.

English settlers in America also brought with them the name for a large deer with grand antlers: the elk. Elk inhabited northern regions of Europe, and the name *elk* had come into English from Old Norse. The North American animal that the English called an elk was, in fact, an elk. But it also came to be known as a moose. The name *moose* came from an Indian word that meant "bark stripper" or "wood eater." Trees bare of bark were a sign that this deer had enjoyed a meal.

The settlers also used the name *elk* to refer to another, slightly smaller North American deer. But this deer was not, in fact, an elk. Its Shawnee Indian name, *wapiti* ("white-tailed rump"), fits the animal better. Today the name *wapiti* (WOP-uh-tee) is sometimes used interchangeably with *American elk.*

As usual, the scientific names help to keep things orderly. The moose is *Alces alces*; the wapiti is *Cervus canadensis*; the elk of northern Europe and Asia is *Alces alces.*

BUFFALO DUSK

The buffaloes are gone.
And those who saw the buffaloes are gone.
Those who saw the buffaloes by thousands and how they pawed the
*   prairie sod into dust with their hoofs, their great heads down pawing*
*   on in a great pageant of dusk,*
Those who saw the buffaloes are gone.
And the buffaloes are gone.

CARL SANDBURG

The American West was once home to vast herds of grazing buffalo. They are large mammals with shaggy manes, huge heads, and short horns. The Plains Indians were famous for their buffalo-hunting skills; the flesh and fur and sinews of the great beasts were vital to the Indians' way of life. Then

111

came the pioneers, the railroads, and settlement. The buffalo—which once numbered in the millions—were almost wiped out. Today, in spite of their reduced numbers, the buffalo survive. They remain a strong symbol of the old West.

Eighteen states, from New York to Minnesota to Wyoming, have cities named Buffalo. Countless other places in the United States include the word *Buffalo* in their names. All those names reveal how important the buffalo once was in America. They also reveal a mislabeling practice, since the American buffalo is not really a buffalo at all.

The word *buffalo* comes from the Portuguese *bufalo*. That name, in turn, comes from an older Greek word, *boufalos*, meaning "wild ox." Europeans used the name *bufalo* to describe the African or Asian ox, animals such as the water buffalo (also called a carabao) and the Cape buffalo. These Asian and African buffalo are smaller, weaker, and quite different-looking from the American buffalo. The American animal is correctly called a bison (BY-sun, or sometimes BY-zun). The word *bison* has Latin and Germanic roots. It referred to a European wild ox. European bison were once wild and plentiful. Today they survive in just one herd, restricted to a game preserve between Poland and Russia. The European bison is also more accurately called a wisent (VEE-zent); the pronunciation comes from German. Perhaps you can see and hear the relationship between the words *wisent* and *bison*.

The wisent is sometimes incorrectly called an aurochs (AWR-ahks); can you hear the *ox* in the name? The true aurochs is extinct. Scientists believe that it was the ancestor of domestic cattle in Africa, Europe, and Asia. They have therefore given it an important-sounding name, *Bos primigenius* (roughly translated as "earliest ox-cow-bull").

By now oxlike creatures called bison and Cape buffalo and water buffalo and carabao and wisents and aurochses may be kicking up clouds of confusion in your head. Just one thing more. A new animal has recently come on the scene, as a result of human activities. Ranchers have crossed the American buffalo with domestic cattle and come up with . . . can you guess? *catalo* (or *beefalo*).

English-speaking settlers were not the only nonnatives to label (or mislabel) New World animals. Some American animals were named by Spanish-speaking people. Spanish influences on language in the United States were strongest in the areas of Spanish settlement—Florida and the Southwest. That is why, for example, a small burrowing creature of the southern United States is called an armadillo. The Spanish word *armado*, meaning "armored" or "plated," plus a suffix meaning "small," provided a perfect name for this mammal. Bony plates combine to form a jointed shell for the armadillo, so it does appear to be wearing a suit of armor.

According to one story, a group of Spanish explorers was investigating a swampy Florida waterway. All at once, a long, monstrous thing slithered into the water from the bank where it had been resting. One Spaniard spotted it and called out, *"El lagarto!"* (That's Spanish for "The lizard!") The story may not be true, but the name stuck, with a few changes in sound: *alligator*. The name is not as suitable as the armadillo's, however. Although it is a reptile, the alligator is not a lizard.

The Nahuatl Indians of Mexico used the name *coyotl* for a wolflike, wily animal. The Mexican Spanish changed it to the name we know today, *coyote*. Its two present pronunciations show that the word is still changing among North American speakers; some say *ky-OH-tee*, others prefer *KY-oht*.

The Spanish conquistadores of the sixteenth century brought the horse to the New World. Horses soon became necessary to American life, first among the Plains Indians and later among cattle ranchers and cowboys. Many cowboy- and horse-related terms come from Spanish. The name *palomino*, for example, comes from the Spanish word for "dove." It refers to the dovelike golden-tan color of the horse we call a palomino.

When the conquistadores left, many of their horses remained. The descendants of those horses reverted to their wild habits and roamed free. Mexican associations called *mestas* were formed to capture the stray horses and divide them among association members. The horses without masters belonged to the *mesta*, and so were called *mesteños* (mes-TEN-yohs). In American Spanish, the horses became known as *mestengos*. Wild horses still range over areas of the American West. We call them mustangs.

Animal names have been on the move for a long time. Whether they have been brought to us from foreign lands or by foreign speakers, they have traveled to the same place. They belong to English now.

From One Animal to Another

During the Middle Ages, Europeans were just beginning to learn about the strange beasts that lived in faraway lands. Foreign travelers told marvelous stories (at times adding fanciful details to the facts) about animals they had seen. An unusually tall beast lived in Africa, it was said, with a head like a camel's and spots like a leopard's. Described in that way, the animal could be only one thing: a camelopard. And so it was called for hundreds of years. Today we call the camelopard by a different name, one of Arabic origin: *giraffe*. The scientific name for the animal, however, incorporates both versions: *Giraffa camelopardis.*

Trying to come up with names for animals, people have naturally compared the new and unfamiliar beasts with better-known ones. If an animal resembles a camel and a leopard, well, why *not* call it a camelopard? The name *leopard* itself is the result of such a combination. English-speaking people used to call any large wild cat, such as a panther, by one name—*pard.* A leo-pard, or leopard, was thought to be half lion (*leo* is Latin for lion) and half pard.

It does seem fitting to call a large and deep-voiced frog a *bullfrog*, or a whiskered fish a *catfish*, or a ferocious beetle a *tiger beetle.* But sometimes our tendency to combine can lead us astray.

Perhaps you can see the *lion* in chame**leon.** The name for this lizard comes from the Greek word for "ground lion," not necessarily because it lives on the ground (most chameleons are tree dwellers), but because of its dwarfish, close-to-the-ground size. Chameleons are probably best noted for their ability to change their colors and patterns, which include green, yellow, dark brown, whitish, and spotted. These changes enable them to blend in with their surroundings and hide from predators such as snakes and birds. Even more distinctive, however, are the chameleon's eyes, which bulge out of its head and swivel in all directions, separately from each other. And its sticky-tipped tongue, designed for catching insects, bursts out of its mouth to a distance that can be longer than its own body. The chameleon's characteristics may make it a fascinating creature, but not exactly a *leonine* ("lionlike") one.

The chameleon is not the only animal capable of color change. Other lizards can change color, and so can some fish and the octopus. But for some reason, the ability to change colors and blend in with one's surroundings is most strongly associated with the chameleon. That association is behind an extended meaning for the chameleon's name:

"I don't know whether Wiley is with us or against us."
"I can't tell either. He's such a chameleon."

Any person whose opinions and alliances are not steady, who is unreliable and changeable, may be called a chameleon.

* * *

116

The pig was one of the first animals to be domesticated by human beings. Pigs and people have lived together for a long, long time. It's no wonder that an animal in need of a name has often been forced into a comparison with the familiar pig or hog. The groundhog and the guinea pig, which were mentioned in the last section, are two examples. The hedgehog is another.

If the hedgehog is known at all to American children, it is probably by way of stories imported from England, such as those in the popular Beatrix Potter books. The hedgehog is a character in animal stories for European children because it is a well-known European animal. In the New World, however, it is unknown. The *hog* in the animal's name is based on its somewhat piglike snout, but the hedgehog is not a member of the pig family. The *hedge* part of its name may have come from hedgerows (rows of shrubs and bushes), where it was often seen. It is more likely, however, that the *hedge* comes from the animal's own similarity to a hedge. Because its back is covered with stiff, sharp spines, the animal does seem like a thorny shrub. When in danger from an attacker, the hedgehog rolls itself into a ball of spines.

A different spiny animal is more familiar to North American children. From the Italian word *porcospino* and the Old French *porc-espin*, English speakers came up with *porcupine.* All three names mean "spiny pig" or "quill pig." Like the guinea pig, the porcupine is actually a rodent, not a pig. Its stubby legs and its snout do look piglike, and the porcupine has been known to crash through the underbrush like a wild pig.

But there the resemblance ends. To threaten a stranger, the porcupine growls and stamps, and stiffens the 30,000 needle-sharp quills on its body. It will use those quills, too, lunging at anyone or anything that comes too close. The quills break off easily, embedding themselves painfully and memorably into the victim. The *pig* part of the porcupine's name may be misleading, but the *spiny* part does make its point.

Try to picture this water mammal: It has a beaklike snout and a streamlined, torpedo-shaped body that is ideal for speedy swimming. It travels in groups. It is known for its friendliness to human beings and its intelligence.

Now, if you had to think of a name for this mammal, would you call it a pig fish? Maybe not, but that is in fact what we call the animal. The Old French word for "pig fish" was *porpois.* In English it is *porpoise.*

Dutch settlers in South Africa met a burrowing mammal that relied on a steady diet of termites. It had a stout and hairy body, a two-foot tail, a long and tubelike snout, four thin legs, tall upright ears, a foot-long tongue, and very sharp claws. The settlers gave the animal a name. They applied the first part of the name, *aard,* meaning "earth," because the animal was an expert digger. They applied the second part of the name, *vark,* meaning "pig," because . . . well, people do seem to see pigs everywhere. Even in creatures as unusual as aardvarks.

The ancient Egyptians are generally credited with domesticating a wild North African cat and breeding the ancestors of today's pet, *Felis catus*. (From the Latin word for "cat," *felis*, comes our word *feline*, which refers to cats or catlike characteristics.) During the thousands of years that cats and people have known each other, the cat has played the roles of mouse catcher, object of worship, symbol of the devil, companion of witches, and household pet. It has also been a source of animal names.

Our pet tabby and the leaf-chomping larva of a butterfly or moth may not seem to have anything in common. But from the Old French word *catepelose*, "hairy cat," creeps our *caterpillar*. Caterpillars do look hairy, but feline? . . .

Caterpillars come in countless forms. When a name for one was needed, comparison was the handy method. For example, you may have seen a fat *woolly bear caterpillar* inching along a twig. When you think about its name, this larva is actually a woolly-bear-hairy-cat. What strange thing could it possibly change into in its adult stage? Why, a *tiger moth*.

The polecat is not a cat. It is a small mammal of Europe and northern Africa, related to a weasel. The *pole* in its name may have come from an Old French word for "hen," not because polecats look like hens but because they like to steal and eat chickens. The polecat gives off a bad odor, which is probably why in some regions of North America an unrelated but smelly animal, the skunk, is called a polecat.

Ancient Romans and Europeans tamed the wild polecat. They domesticated a breed that came to be called a ferret. (The name *ferret* was based on a Latin word for "thief.") They used ferrets for killing rats and for hunting rabbits. It was the ferret's notable skill at digging out hidden prey that suggested another meaning for its name. We use the phrase *to ferret out* ("We'll try to ferret out the smugglers and bring them to justice") when we describe our own search efforts.

North America does have a ferret of its own, a species related to the Old World polecat. This animal, the wild black-footed ferret of the Great Plains, is extremely rare today. It is disappearing because its main source of food is not as available as it once was. That source of food is another western mammal, the prairie dog.

As you can probably guess by now, the prairie dog is not a dog. It is a rodent, a member of the squirrel family. Like another American mammal, the buffalo, prairie dogs once lived on the plains by the millions—in numbers so high they are hard to imagine.

Even more remarkable than their once-astonishing numbers is the prairie dogs' way of life. These burrowing animals live in vast underground communities. They build networks of tunnels that can stretch for miles, with multiple entrances, flood-control constructions, and built-in temperature and moisture regulators. Their underground passageways, which can reach fourteen feet below the surface, include food-storage rooms and nesting chambers carpeted with grass. In 1901 a naturalist reported visiting a prairie dog town that was 250 miles long, 100 miles wide, and home to *400 million* prairie dogs. Because the land that prairie dogs need was also wanted by human builders, prairie dog towns were purposely destroyed.

The prairie dog has survived. Today prairie dog towns still exist, although on a smaller scale. They can be found from Texas north to Canada.

Surely *prairie dog* is not the most descriptive name for these construction engineers. Dogs, after all, are not known for their refined digging skills. The name comes from the method that these social animals use to communicate with each other: They bark.

Have you ever seen a fox flying through the air? Neither has anyone else. But the tropical animals known as flying foxes take to the air by the thousands every night, hunting for fruit. During the day, they sleep in crowded colonies, hanging upside down from tree branches. They wrap their wings around themselves as they sleep. When spread apart, those wings may span three feet. Unusual qualities for a fox, don't you agree?

Yes, but these animals are not foxes. They are giant bats, sometimes called fox bats. Their name was suggested by their foxlike faces. The genus label, *Pteropus*, which means "wing footed," describes a more important feature. Bats are the only mammals with wings. Their wings are thin membranes connecting their fingers, sides, and legs.

Even if you have never seen a river horse or a whale horse up close, you probably know what these water mammals look like. You may not recognize the names, however. Neither animal is a horse.

From the Greek words *hippos ho potamios*, "horse of the river," comes our name for the nasty-tempered, five-ton beast of African rivers, the *hippopotamus*. This animal spends most of its time submerged in the water, with only its eyes and nostrils protruding above the surface. When seen from that limited viewpoint, the animal does resemble a horse, but just barely.

Because it has huge tusks, the whale horse was once also known as a whale elephant. The preferred name comes from the Norsemen, who knew these Arctic sea mammals well. They called them *hvalross*, "whale horse," and English speakers have adapted that name to its present form: *walrus*.

What do you think a pebble worm looks like? A slimy pinkish thing that drags its rubbery body amid the pebbles under your feet? Guess again.

The creature described by the Greeks as "worm (or serpent) of the pebbles" is a fearsome reptile of tropical lakes and rivers. It is a powerful swimmer that often floats motionless, with only its eyes and the tip of its snout above the water. It waits and watches for an unwary fish, turtle, bird, or mammal to come near. Then, in a flash, it attacks. Escape from the sharp teeth and mighty jaws is impossible. Some of these reptiles have been known to eat people.

In Greek "worm of the pebbles" is *krokodilos*. (Its name comes from its habit of sunbathing on the shore.) In present-day English, we call the reptile a crocodile.

*　　*　　*

There is an animal called a cowfish. It is neither a cow nor a fish, but a small whale. A sea cow is not a cow, a sea horse is not a horse, and a horseshoe crab is not a crab. The list of not-quite-accurate names for animals goes on. As you have seen, some names are combinations of names of unrelated creatures, such as *camelopard* or *porpoise*. Other names are the result of a comparison with a familiar but unrelated animal, such as *hedgehog*, *flying fox*, or *prairie dog*. In everyday conversation, we prefer to speak of a *porcupine*, and not *Erethizon dorsatum* (the animal with an "irritating back"). But it's good to know that the scientific name is there, just in case we need to be clear about which "spiny pig" we mean.

Plant Names Have Roots, Too

You have seen the scientific names that are used to classify and label animals. Members of the animal kingdom, however, are not the only life forms on earth. Scientific names are also needed for the strange, common, beautiful, ugly, aromatic, smelly, enormous, tiny, healthful, poisonous, and—most of all—*varied* members of the plant kingdom. When it comes to naming plants, English-speaking people have let their imaginations run free. And running close behind is confusion.

Among English-speaking people, it is typical to find a half dozen different names for the same plant, and the same name applied to different plants. Despite this disorder, the popular names for plants can be as fascinating as the plants themselves.

That, of all the floures in the mede,
Thanne love I most these floures
white and rede,
Swyche as men calle dayesyes in oure
toun.

GEOFFREY CHAUCER

Chaucer's Middle English becomes in modern English:

That of all the flowers in the meadow,
I love most these flowers
white and red,
Such as men call daisies in our
town.

The earlier spelling of *daisies* gives a hint about the origin of the flower's name. Another Middle English spelling gives an even better clue: *dayeseye*. This "day's-eye" is not the flower that North Americans know well (the one with a yellow center and white rays). North Americans would call Chaucer's flowers English daisies. The rays of English daisies may indeed be "white and rede" (and pink, too). The common American daisy is sometimes called an oxeye daisy, which means that its common name is really ox-eye-day's-eye.

The name *daisy* describes not just one plant but a vast family of plants. Daisies make up the largest family of flowering plants in the world. Scientists have labeled the family *Compositae* because the flowers are actually composites—they are composed of many small flowers growing together. In typical daisies, the flat rays surrounding the center disk are actually separate flowers. And the center disk is made of tiny flowers, too.

Does a daisy look like a "day's-eye"? The name does seem to fit, especially when it refers to a daisy with rays that curve inward as night falls. The bright-yellow sunlike disk is then hidden. It is revealed in the morning, just like the sun, the "eye of day."

In North America, the names we have given to various plants of the daisy family are wonderfully descriptive. Consider, for example, *sneezeweed* (guess what's supposed to happen when you sniff it), *boneset* (parts of this plant were thought useful in mending broken bones), *feverfew* (this was once used medicinally to reduce a fever), *sticktight* (its prickly seeds stick to the fur or clothing of passersby), and *devil's paintbrush* (this has a deep-orange, fiery color).

An Old English name for any plant was *wort*. Now we find *wort* as part of many plant names, including the daisy family members *golden ragwort*, which has tattered, ragged leaves, and *feverwort*, which was once used in medicine.

The word *bane* is frequently found in plant names. It means "the cause of harm or death." The daisylike fleabane, for example, was once believed to drive away fleas.

Here is a list of other daisy family members. How do you think each got its name? *Cat's-ear*, *catfoot*, *field pussytoes*, *goldenrod, silverrod, blazing star, sun god, yellow goatsbeard, hairy lettuce, pearly everlasting, dusty miller, black-eyed Susan, Barbara's buttons, stinking groundsel.*

Members of the daisy family are not the only plants with flowers that open and close each day. The morning glory family includes two hundred species, growing all over the world. The petals of morning glories fold up in the evening. When the sky brightens again, bell-shaped flowers unfold to greet the day, as if ringing out the good news with a burst of color—white, pink, red, purple, blue. *Morning glory.* A lovely name.

But not everyone thinks morning glories are lovely. The plants are often trailing or twining vines. They can form a dense tangle on the ground, which chokes crops. These not-so-glorious qualities of some morning glories explain their other, not-so-poetic name: *bindweed.*

Thick white juice oozes from the broken stems of plants of another family. It's easy to see where the family name *milkweed* comes from. Milkweed also has distinctive seed pods. Because the seeds are attached to tufts of silky threads, another common name for some of these plants is *silkweed.*

There are about one hundred different species within the milkweed family. Most are native to the New World. The scientific name for the milkweed family is a mouthful: *Asclepiadeaceae.* It is taken from the name of the Greek god of healing, Asclepius (uh-SKLEE-pee-us), whose medical powers were thought to be so great that he could bring the dead back to life.

126

The connection between medicine and milkweed is clear. Throughout history herbalists (people who treat illness with specially collected and prepared plants) have used plants of the milkweed family to make medicine.

Like Asclepius, other characters from classical mythology appear in the names for plants. Some myths make Asclepius the son of Apollo, an important Greek and Roman god. Apollo was associated with archery, music, and healing. Apollo was also called by the name Paion, which had been used earlier by the Greeks to refer to "the healer of the gods." Paion, it was told, was the discoverer of a beautiful flower that could cure illness. The flower is named after Paion and has come into English as *peony* (PEE-uh-nee).

According to legend, Apollo was throwing a discus when he accidentally killed a beautiful young man called Hyacinthus. Feeling great sadness, Apollo caused a flower to spring from the dead youth's blood. The plant became known as a hyacinth.

Our modern hyacinth is not the plant of Greek legend. We have borrowed only the name. It is not clear exactly what the ancient Greek hyacinth looked like—some say it might have been what we now call an iris. The name *iris* also comes from Greek mythology.

The Greek word for rainbow was *iris.* It was also the name of a minor goddess. Iris was a messenger of the gods. The bridge she used to travel to earth was a rainbow, and she was known as the goddess of the rainbow. We use the word *iris* to refer to the colored portion of the eye, and to a family of plants with colorful flowers. Just like the rainbow, irises range in color from red to orange to yellow to blue to violet.

Another Greek myth tells of a young man named Narcissus who was extraordinarily handsome. No wonder the mountain nymph Echo fell in love with him. But Narcissus would have nothing to do with her. He ignored Echo so cruelly that she stopped eating. She wasted away until only her voice remained. (Her voice is the *echo* so often heard in the mountains.) The goddess of vengeance stepped in to punish Narcissus. He paused by a pool of water one day, glanced in, and was made to fall in love with what he saw there—his own reflection. Now it was Narcissus' turn to pine away for love of someone he could not have. As he died, he was changed into a flower: the narcissus. The myth of Narcissus is also the source of the name for a human trait. Excessive vanity or self-admiration is called narcissism.

Helios was the Greek sun god. His love for the ocean nymph Clytie was short-lived even though her love was strong and permanent. When Helios abandoned her, Clytie pined away and died. She was changed into a flower. The flower known as the *heliotrope* (Greek for "turn toward sun") turns to face the sun as it travels across the sky each day.

Today we still call some plants heliotropes. Our more usual label for the plants that turn toward the sun is *sunflower*. The scientific name for the common sunflower is *Helianthus annuus* ("yearly sun flower"). The Greek *helios* can still be seen in the name.

Venus's basin, Venus's-comb, Venus's looking-glass, Venus's-hair,

Venus's-slipper. Flowers have long symbolized love, romance, and courtship. It is not surprising that we find the name of the Roman goddess of love and beauty, Venus, in the names of plants. Another plant must be added to the list. The *Venus's-flytrap* may not make you think of love. It is one of the so-called meat-eating plants. To the insects that the plant devours, however, the Venus's-flytrap is certainly attractive . . . at first.

Question: What's the smallest room in the world?
Answer: A mushroom.

Did people once believe that this common fungus looked like a room of mush? Is that why they named it a mushroom?

No. The word *mushroom* illustrates an important point about language: Words change in sound and spelling over time. In Middle English, the word sometimes appeared in writing as *muscheron.* It had come into English by way of Old French (*mousseron*) from a Latin word related to *moss.* Before our present pronunciation and spelling were settled upon, a mushroom was sometimes called a mushrump. So you see, *mush* and *room* have nothing to do with the meaning of *mushroom.* The source of the name of a similar but inedible fungus, the toadstool, is easier to see. It does look like a stool. The toadstool was not a stool for toads to sit on, however. Toads were thought to be poisonous, and so was the fungus.

In Middle English, the flower called a dent-de-lion got its name from the French words meaning "tooth of lion."

The leaves have sharp, toothlike notches. (You might say they have in**dent**ations in them—do you see that Latin root meaning "tooth"?) Over time, the dent-de-lion has become our familiar lawn weed, the dandelion.

The French *herbe de la pensée* ("flower of thought") was long called a pensée in England. The flower itself did not look thoughtful, or **pens**ive (see a Latin root again?), but was exchanged by lovers as a token of thought or remembrance. Over hundreds of years, we have given the French word a comfortably English sound: *pansy*.

The large, brightly colored flower of the plant called a tulip resembles a turban. A turban is a headdress made with a winding scarf. It originated in the Middle East. The tulip was, in fact, named after the turban. Both *tulip* and *turban* come from a Turkish word for *turban*, a word that sounds like TOOL-*bend*. The flower and the headdress have different names in English because they traveled different routes from the Turkish source. You can see the relationship between the words more clearly if you look at former English versions of each. In English the tulip used to be called a tulipan. The turban used to be called a tulban. *Tulipan. Tulban.* You can just about see and hear that shared Turkish root.

Like the tulip, which was native to Asia, other plants that were becoming known to Europeans had to be given names. The native names were often passed on, undergoing changes along the way.

The native Nahuatl language of Mexico had a word for a plant that Europeans had never seen before: *tomatl*. Traveling through Spanish, the word, along with the plant, came to us as *tomato.*

When Christopher Columbus made the famous error of thinking that he was in the East Indies when he was actually in the Western Hemisphere, the so-called Indians he met included the Taino. The Taino people of the West Indies were eventually wiped out by the Spanish conquerors. But fragments of their language survive. The Taino had a name for a New World plant that was soon to become a staple food in Europe. Passing through Spanish, the Taino *batata* became *potato.*

The Taino word *mahiz* described another New World plant. The word traveled through Spanish to become the English word *maize.* In the United States, the word *corn* is used to name the plant. But in Great Britain, corn is used as a general name for any cereal crop (wheat, rye, and oats are all called corn). The word *maize* remains much more common in England than in the United States.

Scientists who study plants are called botanists. When early botanists began to travel to distant lands on collecting trips, they discovered many new forms of plant life. The new plants needed names. What better way to show respect for a fellow botanist than by giving a plant that botanist's name!

When a seventeenth-century French botanist returned to Europe after exploring the Caribbean and Brazil, he published a book with descriptions of more than one hundred new plant groups. He named one of his discoveries after Pierre Magnol, a famous French botany teacher. The family of plants *Magnoliaceae* includes the trees and shrubs of the genus *Magnolia*.

A Spanish botanist discovered a plant growing in the high regions of Mexico and Central America. He named the plant after Andreas Dahl, an eighteenth-century Swedish botanist. Today the best place to see the beautiful flower called the *dahlia* is in a florist's shop.

Michel Bégon (1638–1710) was the French governor of a Caribbean colony that is now the Dominican Republic. He was also an amateur botanist, and his name appears within the name of a popular plant, the *begonia*.

Johann Gottfried Zinn (1727–1759) was a German botanist. In his honor, we have the *zinnia*. If you remember the name of another German botanist, Leonhard *Fuchs* (1501–1566), you may be able to master the tricky spelling of the word *fuchsia* (FYOO-shuh). The fuchsia is a shrub with colorful flowers; the bright reddish-purple color called fuchsia is named after the flower.

You might well think that the word *garden* is the source of the name for the lovely, fragrant *gardenia*. In a sense you are right. The plant is named for Dr. Alexander Garden, an eighteenth-century Scottish naturalist who lived in the colony of South Carolina.

Joel Poinsett (1779–1851) played several roles as statesman and diplomat in the developing nation of the United States. Poinsett traveled widely, and like many educated people of his day, he was an amateur naturalist. From a shrub he discovered in Mexico, Poinsett developed a plant that is now known popularly as the *poinsettia.*

At times botanists have chosen to honor people outside their own community of botanists and naturalists. In the early nineteenth century, a Philadelphian named Caspar Wistar was a medical teacher, an outspoken opponent of slavery, and a leading citizen. An English botanist lived for a while in Philadelphia, came to know of Wistar, and named a flowering shrub after him. The botanist also made a small spelling change that has caused confusion ever since: *wisteria* (or, as some prefer, *wistaria*).

About 150 years ago, an Austrian botanist decided to name the California redwood trees after one of the best-known American Indians of his time. The American Indian was a Cherokee man known as Sequoyah (seh-ᴋᴡᴏʜ-yuh), and the grand evergreens are commonly called sequoias. Their scientific names are *Sequoia sempervirens* ("ever-green sequoia," also known as the redwood) and *Sequoia gigantea* ("giant sequoia," also known as the big tree). Sequoyah was not a botanist; he never even traveled to California and never saw the magnificent trees that bear his name. But he had done something remarkable for his people, the Cherokee, and his achievement had captured the attention of many white Americans and Europeans.

Sequoyah spoke only Cherokee, and the Cherokee people (like all native peoples north of Mexico) had never had a written language. Despite his lack of experience with any writing system, Sequoyah singlehandedly created a syllabary, a kind of alphabet in which symbols represent spoken syllables. Sequoyah spent twelve years creating his syllabary of the Cherokee language. Because the system was a clear one, a learner could master it in days and then teach others. That is why the Cherokee were the first Indian nation to become literate. Sequoyah solved a monumentally complicated problem by himself, and his solution was ingenious and practical. His lone twelve-year labor can only be called extraordinary.

The names of people show up not only in names for fragrant flowers and awe-inspiring trees but also in other English words . . . as you'll see in the next chapter.

V

Eponyms

From Name to Word

What's your favorite ride at the amusement park? The roller coaster? The merry-go-round? The whip? The Ferris wheel? It's easy to see where the names for the first three rides came from—those names describe what happens to you (and your stomach) when you climb aboard. The fourth name— Ferris wheel—is different. Although it is sometimes spelled with a small *f*, *ferris wheel*, the capital *F* in its more common spelling is a clue: The Ferris wheel is named after someone.

The someone was an American engineer, George W. Gale Ferris of Galesburg, Illinois. Ferris lived from 1859 to 1896, a period in which the world gloried in impressive feats of engineering, like the grand Eiffel Tower in Paris and the Brooklyn Bridge in New York. Ferris built his first wheel for the World's Columbian Exhibition in Chicago in 1893. It was as tall as a twenty-story building, and each of its huge cars carried forty passengers. A century later, only two or three of us sit in each car, and though we don't climb nearly as high as those first passengers, we still enjoy the view. And we still call the thing a Ferris wheel.

When something—an object, an idea, a behavior—is named after a person, the resulting word is *eponymous* (ih-PAHN-ih-mus), from the Greek word "to name." Dictionaries will tell you that the term *eponym* (EP-uh-nim) refers to the person for whom the thing is named: Mr. Ferris is an eponym. But in everyday usage, *eponym* refers not just to Mr. Ferris but to the thing named after him: the Ferris wheel.

In certain fields, such as medical science, eponyms are common, even though they are usually not part of ordinary speech. A surgical procedure, a test, a disease, a virus, even a part of an organ may be named after its inventor or discoverer. The bite of a rabid animal need no longer lead to the fatal disease rabies, for example, because of the Pasteur treatment. The treatment is named for the French scientist Louis Pasteur (1822–1895), who first successfully treated rabies. Pasteur's name is also known to anyone who has seen the word *pasteurized* on a milk carton. Pasteur invented the sterilization procedure that still bears his name.

It is possible to make a good guess that a word is derived from a person's name. (Why else would a ride be called a Ferris wheel rather than something more descriptive—say, a drop-around or a wheel-winder?) A quick check in a dictionary can verify the guess.

If you've ever looked at the AM and FM bands of a radio, you've probably noticed the letters MHz and kHz. Those letters refer to the frequencies of electromagnetic waves received by your radio, measured in cycles per second. One million cycles per second is a megahertz (MHz), and one thousand cycles per second is a kilohertz (kHz). *Mega* and *kilo* are familiar prefixes (*mega* means "million," *kilo* means "thousand"), but where did the *hertz* come from? It came from Heinrich Rudolf Hertz, a young German physicist who worked on electromagnetism during the late nineteenth century.

The nineteenth century witnessed the blossoming of the new science of physics. Sound, light, magnetism, electricity—relationships between energy and matter—all were being explored and put to use. One discovery about electrical energy is shown in this formula, learned by all beginning physics students today:

$$V = A \times \Omega$$

The *V* stands for *volt*, which measures electromotive force; the *A* stands for *amp* (short for *ampere*), which measures current; and the symbol Ω is the Greek letter omega, which stands for *ohm*, a measure of resistance to current flow. *Volts*, *amps*, and *ohms* are terms used daily by everyone who works with electricity, from car mechanics to electrical engineers. And the word *watt*, which names the unit of electrical power, is known by anyone who has ever looked at a light bulb. All these terms come from names belonging to people.

Count Allesandro Volta (1745–1827) was an Italian physicist

and the inventor of the first battery, which he called a voltaic pile. In those days of candlelight and horse-drawn carriages, Volta could not possibly have imagined the nine-*volt* batteries tucked into a multitude of flashlights or the high-*voltage* wires strung across our landscape.

Living in Volta's time was a French mathematician and physicist who was making discoveries about electricity and the earth's magnetic field. His name was André-Marie Ampère (1775–1836), and a shortened form of his name, *amp*, is mentioned today whenever the intensity of electrical current is discussed.

Georg Simon Ohm (1787–1854) was a brilliant German physicist, whose contributions included the discovery of the mathematical law of electrical currents, which is known as Ohm's Law. (The formula appears four paragraphs before this one.)

James Watt was a Scottish inventor who lived from 1736 to 1819. He invented not only machines but also a word to describe their ability: *horsepower*. His primary work was making mathematical instruments, though he is probably best known today for his effort to refine the steam engine, a machine that was to change the industrial world and the course of history.

When a current of one ampere is passed through a resistance of one ohm for one second, the work done is called a *joule*. The measurement unit known as a joule was named for James Prescott Joule (1818–1889), a British physicist. Scientists and engineers need to think of work as a quantity that can be measured—the joule is a handy unit. So is the *newton*, a measure of force.

The newton is named for one of history's great geniuses, the English scientist Sir Isaac Newton (1642–1727). Today schoolchildren may know Newton's name from the amusing legend of his discovery of the theory of gravity. It is told that he sat beneath an apple tree, felt an apple plop onto his head, and came up with a good explanation. Actually, Sir Isaac Newton came up with so many good explanations in the studies of mathematics, mechanics, gravitation, and philosophy that he is an eponym for a whole branch of science—Newtonian physics.

The nineteenth century was an era of invention and discovery. A German student of engineering, born in 1858, invented an improvement to the internal combustion engine. By the start of the twentieth century, his engine had made him famous. Today every truck driver knows his name (or at least his surname): Rudolf *Diesel*.

When we picture oil wells, we usually see those complicated rigs dotting a landscape of the Middle East or of the American Southwest. Those constructions are called derricks. Though oil derricks are a twentieth-century phenomenon, the word *derrick* has been applied for centuries to a kind of crane used for lifting heavy objects. Engineers are justifiably proud of their derricks. It was an engineer, of sorts, who invented the first one. He was a man known as Derrick, possibly from Holland, who lived in England in the 1600's. Derrick was the chief hangman of England. He hanged criminals and political foes of the English rulers—performing perhaps 3,000 executions. By making changes to the basic gallows structure, Derrick created a new-and-improved version. The word *Derrick* came to be spoken as the name for the gallows itself, and then for the hoisting device that has borne the name since.

Inventors and inventions are not limited to the fields of science and engineering. Consider Jules Leotard, a French acrobat who lived from 1842 to 1870. He invented the flying trapeze. He also invented the costume that made trapeze flying more comfortable: the *leotard*.

Another familiar item of clothing is a button-front sweater called a *cardigan*. Although Cardigan is a county in Wales, the sweater did not originate there. It is named for the nineteenth-century British army officer James Thomas Brudenell, Seventh Earl of Cardigan. Lord Cardigan led British soldiers during the Crimean War (1853–56), and the warm jacket worn by the soldiers became known as a Cardigan jacket.

Speaking of clothing, nobody speaks of pantaloons anymore, though Americans often use the shortened form: *pants*. Until the twentieth century, the word *pants* was frowned upon by editors, who thought it a slang term not fit for print. The form they preferred, *pantaloons*, had already had a long history. *Pantaloons* was derived from the name of a fictional character in European traveling shows that were first performed in the sixteenth century. This form of popular street drama originated in Italy and was known as the *commedia dell'arte* ("comedy of skill").

142

The *commedia dell'arte* had stock characters whom audiences learned to watch for and laugh at. One of these characters was a wealthy but foolish merchant who often served as the butt of jokes. He was old and skinny, and wore a mask with a hooked nose. He always had on a black cape, slippers, and a pair of tight trousers. The character's name was Pantaleone. By the 1600's, the word *Pantaloon* was being used in England to describe fashionable tight-fitting trousers that fastened under the boots.

Until relatively recently, the item of clothing known as knickers was worn by nearly everyone. Boys wore knickers, or knee-length trousers, until they were grown-up enough for long pants. *Knickers* was also the name for a knee-length undergarment worn by women and girls. Like the word *pants*, *knickers* was a shortened form of a fictional character's name. This character's name was Diedrich Knickerbocker, and he appeared in books by the well-known American author Washington Irving. In 1809, Irving published a book in which Diedrich Knickerbocker recounted the history of New York. New York was originally a Dutch settlement, and Knickerbocker was depicted in illustrations wearing the baggy britches worn by Dutch settlers. Starting from the beginning, then, we have gone from *Knickerbocker* to *knickerbockers* to *knickers* to . . . where will it end? Well, there is the basketball team the New York Knickerbockers—familiarly known as the *Knicks*.

Knickers may go in and out of fashion, but chances are good that you have worn a jersey. And chances are even better that you own a pair of jeans. *Jersey* and *jeans* are eponymous words of another sort; they are named not after people but after places.

Jersey is the largest of the Channel Islands that lie between Normandy and England. It has given its name to a breed of dairy cattle and to an article of clothing. *Jersey* was originally applied to a Jersey fisherman's sweater, made of a woolen fabric first knitted by Jersey islanders. It has since been used to name any knitted pullover garment.

Long ago, a heavy cotton fabric was introduced to England from Genoa, Italy, where it was first made. The fabric was known in Middle English as Jene because of its place of origin. Pants made of this fabric are today called jeans.

The name for another item of clothing has entered English much more recently. It, too, was named after a place. The place was a tiny coral island, or atoll, in the Pacific Ocean. The atoll became famous in 1946 as the site of American atomic bomb tests. Back then, the brand-new atom bomb was on everyone's mind, so the name for the island was front-page news. At about the same time, French women began showing up on beaches in extremely skimpy two-piece bathing suits, and the new fashion seemed to hit those beaches with bomblike force. The two news events became connected, and the island of Bikini became the source of the bathing-suit name *bikini*.

Fashions come and go, not only in clothing. Think of how hairstyles change from decade to decade, or even from year to year. The Marquise de Pompadour (1721–64) was a beautiful, intelligent, and influential mistress of King Louis

XV of France. The king had granted her the estate of Pompadour, from which she took her title. Madame de Pompadour was much imitated by the fashionable ladies of the day. Her hair, swept up high on her head, set the style still known as the *pompadour*.

One hundred years later, an American general became an unlikely fashion trendsetter. Ambrose Burnside was born in Indiana in 1824. During the Civil War, he commanded the Union forces in the battles of Petersburg and Fredericksburg. The Union soldiers suffered terrible defeats in those battles, but Burnside is not remembered so much for those failures as for his facial hair. When Burnside later served as a U.S. senator, many women and men admired the magnificent whiskers he grew in front of his ears. Men began to develop their "Burnsides" too. Over time, and through a quirk of language, the name changed to *sideburns*.

The arts have their fashions too. One form of portraiture, still known today, went through a long period of popularity, beginning in the eighteenth century. The portraits were made by first projecting the shadow of a person's profile onto a piece of paper and then tracing its outline. The resulting profile, cut from black paper, was known as a silhouette. Today we use the word *silhouette* to describe not only the art form but any dark shape in outline. Trees may be silhouetted against the evening sky, for example, or suspicious figures may be seen in silhouette, lurking in ill-lit corners.

Étienne de Silhouette (1709–67) was not the originator of the silhouette portrait. He was a French finance minister, a contemporary of Madame de Pompadour. Actually, it was she who helped him gain his official position. Silhouette's job was to rescue the failing French economy, and he used harsh methods: high taxes and limited spending. Such ideas are unpopular in any age, and Silhouette quickly lost his position. But because of his frugal recommendations, any plain or cheap fashion of that time was labeled "à la Silhouette." Some say that the black profile came to be known as a silhouette because it was much cheaper to make than a color painting. Others claim that Silhouette's enemies compared the portrait to Silhouette's own shadowy, insubstantial economic plans. In either case, the name *silhouette* was originally used to disparage. Today that negative association is lost.

The musical arts have also contributed eponyms. A Belgian instrument maker named Adolphe Sax died at the turn of the twentieth century, before the age of jazz. He never heard great jazz artists sweep the emotional scale with an instrument he had invented for marching bands: the *saxophone.*

Helen Porter Armstrong (1861–1931), an Australian opera singer, became the most popular soprano of her time. Her stage name was Nellie Melba. Although Nellie Melba influenced the opera world, it is the food world that has borrowed her name. Two tasty items are eponymous: a fruit-and-ice-cream concoction called *peach melba*, and a dainty cracker called *melba toast.*

The name for another food item is possibly the most often-heard eponym among English-speaking people today. Whether you ask for it with white bread, a pumpernickel roll, or whole-wheat toast; whether you prefer mayonnaise or mustard slathered on it; whether you add lettuce or tomato; whether you fill it with salami, roast beef, turkey, cheese, peanut butter and jelly, or all those things together; you are getting ready to sink your teeth into a *sandwich*. It is not known who actually invented the meal-between-sliced-bread affairs, but John Montagu, the Fourth Earl of Sandwich (1718–92) certainly ate a lot of them. Lord Sandwich ate his beef between slices of bread so that he wouldn't have to sit down to a formal dinner. His mind was often on something that mattered more to him: gambling. His addiction to card games required him to spend hour upon hour at the card table, eating only the special meals that he had ordered his servant to bring to him. Those meals were soon to be known as sandwiches. It is said that Lord Sandwich, in addition to devoting himself to a questionable hobby, was dishonest, disloyal, and not a likable sort of fellow at all. Regardless of what Lord Sandwich's contemporaries thought of him, people today often brighten at the sound of his name. Want a sandwich?

Perhaps you'd like a jumbo sandwich. How about a jumbo burger? Jumbo fries? You can even get jumbo shrimp. The word *jumbo*, meaning "extra large," is eponymous. The original Jumbo was a huge elephant who had lived in the London zoo for many years before being sold in 1882 to the American circus owner P. T. Barnum. Jumbo's name may have come from the shortening of the expression *mumbo-jumbo*, which Europeans thought was an African term. Three years after Jumbo began astounding American viewers with his enormousness, he was struck by a freight train and killed. His skeleton is still housed at the Smithsonian Institution in Washington, D.C.

Another animal has contributed its name to the English language, along with that of an American president. President Theodore Roosevelt enjoyed hunting. While on a hunting trip in the southern United States, he was offered the opportunity to shoot a small bear. The bear had already been captured for him. Roosevelt refused. He enjoyed the hunt, not the simple act of killing. News reporters played up the incident. Rough-and-tough Teddy Roosevelt was too kindhearted, they said, to shoot a helpless bear. Soon after, the small stuffed bears that had long been childhood playthings were given a new name. The name is still used today: *teddy bears.*

Disfavor and Foolishness

How would you like to become eponymous someday and have your name in the dictionary? What would you like to be known for? A scientific invention or discovery? a medical procedure? a tasty food? a wacky item of clothing or hairstyle? a form of art or music? Before you say yes to any of these questions, you should recognize that your name may turn out to have associations different from the ones you hoped for. Consider the intellectually gifted philosopher of the Middle Ages known as John Duns Scotus (1256–1308). The name *Scotus* described him as a "man from Scotland." John Duns Scotus inspired awe in the thinkers of his time because of the strength of his arguments about the nature of Christianity. His followers were called Scotists, Dunsmen, or Dunses. But by the 1500's, these Dunses were behind the times. Their reasoning was considered backward and rigid. Dunses were ridiculed as fools. Now, hundreds of years later, a foolish and ignorant person may still be called a *dunce.*

Dunce has earned its negative connotations through the passage of time. Other eponymous words are born as terms of disparagement or ridicule. In the seventeenth century, a French officer served in the army of King Louis XIV. The officer was known for his harsh and inflexible discipline. He insisted that soldiers spend hours at drill. He demanded obedience and perfection. His name was Jean Martinet. And today any leader, teacher, boss, or baby-sitter who is a *martinet* is likely to be dreaded and despised.

About one hundred fifty years after Martinet, another French soldier became an eponym. The soldier, Nicholas Chauvin, was so devoted to the emperor Napoleon that he looked up to Napoleon as a god to be worshipped. Even when Chauvin retired and was granted only a paltry pension and little recognition for his service, he considered himself well rewarded. Within two decades after Napoleon's defeat at Waterloo, French stage productions began to include a ridiculous character named Chauvin, who was blindly devoted to his leader. Today the word *chauvinist* describes someone who believes too intensely in the superiority of his or her own nation or group. And such an exaggerated belief is called *chauvinism.*

149

Political activists and labor organizers have long tried to get their points across by using an economic weapon known as a *boycott*. If all goes according to the organizers' plan, the public learns of the boycott and refuses to buy any product made by the business being boycotted. The managers of the business, suffering terrible losses, give in to demands, and the boycott ends. Whole nations may be victims of a boycott. In 1767, for example, Britain imposed taxes on goods exported to its American colonies, and radical colonists tried to enforce a boycott of British imports. They didn't call their acts of resistance a boycott, however, since that word had not yet been invented. They called their activities nonimportation agreements. Like most boycotts, it was only partly successful. When it comes to politics, widespread agreement is not common. Such agreement is necessary if a boycott is to succeed.

One boycott that had dramatic success took place in 1880 in County Mayo, Ireland. A retired army captain farmed land and also served as agent for the owner of land that was worked by tenant farmers. Two poor harvests had left the tenant farmers without funds, but the agent refused to lower their rents. The local peasants and shopkeepers banded together to shun the agent. He received threatening letters. His servants left him. His crops had to be harvested under armed guards. Eventually the tenants won their case, and the land agent left the country. The agent's name was Captain Charles Cunningham Boycott, and shortly after Boycott was successfully shunned, the verb *to boycott* was born.

Thomas Bowdler (1754–1825) was an English physician

who believed that everyone should be able to read the works of England's greatest dramatist, William Shakespeare. Bowdler also believed that in order for everyone to have that opportunity, Shakespeare's language needed to be cleaned up. After all, Shakespeare had included all sorts of characters in his plays—not only loving families and patriotic kings and queens, but also murderers, liars, thieves, drunkards, fools, and prostitutes. And Shakespeare's characters made earthy, and often comical, references to body functions and sexual activity. Shakespeare's audiences loved to laugh at those lines, but two hundred years later, Thomas Bowdler was troubled by such language. As he explained in his edited ten-volume version of Shakespeare's works, published in 1818, "nothing is added to the original text; but those words and expressions are omitted which cannot with propriety be read aloud in a family."

Bowdler's *The Family Shakespeare* may actually have been "corrected" by Bowdler's sister, Harriet. But it would have been most unseemly to have a woman's name on the work. If Harriet had been credited with the task, then everyone would have known that a *woman*—someone too delicate even to hear a lewd remark—had not only heard a few but had been busily hunting through Shakespeare's plays for all the naughty parts she could find. In any case, it was Thomas Bowdler who earned the credit for this labor of dubious value. He also became an eponym.

Eleven years after his death, the word *bowdlerize* was first used to describe a form of censorship in which an author's words are changed or removed so that the pure of heart may not be offended.

The Reverend Dr. William Archibald Spooner (1844–1930) was an English clergyman noted for his slips of the tongue. His peculiarity was the switching of letters or syllables of words. The results often got a laugh. Instead of saying, "Is this pew occupied?" for example, Rev. W. A. Spooner asked the much odder question, "Is this pie occupewed?" His "May I show you to your seat?" became "May I sew you to your sheet?" His sermon referred to the Lord not as a *loving shepherd* but as a *shoving leopard.* We all make such accidental slips occasionally. But it is also fun to make up *spoonerisms* on purpose: Spoonerisms can found sunny to the ear.

Another comical misuse of language is called a *malapropism.* It is named for Mrs. Malaprop, who was not a real person but a character in a play. The play was *The Rivals*, a comedy by the English playwright Richard Sheridan (1751–1816). Sheridan based the name Malaprop on the French expression *mal à propos*, "out of place."

Sheridan understood what writers of comedies have known since comedy writing began: To make fun of a character's ignorance and grand pretensions, have him or her use big words incorrectly.

Mrs. Malaprop's unwitting substitutions included *preposition* for *proposition, accommodation* for *recommendation*, and *illegible* for *ineligible.* She advised her niece to *illiterate* a fellow from memory, when she meant *obliterate.* Later she said, "I thought she had *persisted* from corresponding"—*desisted* was the sensible

152

word. In what became the most famous malapropism of the play, she referred to an "*allegory* on the banks of the Nile." She was probably thinking of an alligator.

The Greeks

In Chapter IV, in the section "Plant Names Have Roots, Too," you read about hyacinths, heliotropes, and other plants named after characters of Greek mythology. Other figures from ancient Greece—both real and fictional—have given their names to English.

When we hear the wail of a fire-engine siren, we rarely consider that the first *sirens* were mythological sea nymphs. The Greek word *seiren*, meaning "entangler," was used to describe sea creatures that were part bird and part woman. Sirens were noted for their songs, which had such power of enchantment that anyone who heard them could do nothing but listen. The listeners, who were usually sailors, would find their way to the sirens' island and die of starvation and exposure on the beach. In the ancient tale the *Odyssey*, by the Greek poet Homer, the hero Odysseus ordered his sailors to stop their ears with wax when their ship neared the sirens. Odysseus had himself tied to the mast—he thus listened to the sirens' song without being able to act on the urge to jump overboard.

It is said that real-life sailors sometimes thought that the mammals known as sea cows were beautiful mermaids. If you've ever seen a sea cow, such as a manatee, you might

153

wonder just how long those sailors had been at sea. Manatees are not exactly alluring beauties. Still, the order of sea mammals that includes sea cows is called *Sirenia.*

The tale of Odysseus is the source of other eponyms. The word *odyssey* itself, based on the Greek hero's name, has traveled into English. An odyssey is a long and adventure-filled journey.

When Odysseus left the Greek kingdom of Ithaca, he entrusted his household to the care of a friend. This friend was an old and wise man named Mentor. Odysseus also left behind his son, Telemachus, to be guided by the wisdom of Mentor. The goddess Athena offered advice to Telemachus, too, and when she did, she disguised herself as Mentor. Mentor (whether himself or Athena) was a loyal adviser, a selfless and wise teacher, someone we'd all like to have around today to guide us through difficult times. Actually, some of us are lucky enough to know such teachers. We call them *mentors.*

Odysseus had left his home to fight the Trojan War. The Trojan War was an actual event made famous centuries later in an epic poem called the *Iliad,* also credited to the poet Homer. Among the heroes of Greece and Troy described in the *Iliad* was a Greek herald named Stentor. When Stentor made an announcement, everyone knew it, because his voice was as loud as fifty men shouting together. Today loud speeches are given in *stentorian* tones.

Centuries after the Trojan War, the Greek city-states of Athens and Sparta fought a long and bitter war. Sparta was ruled by several powerful military generals. Athens was a democracy. Sparta eventually won the war, probably because Spartans valued success in battle above all else, including life. Newborn Spartans were bathed in icy streams to toughen them. Spartan boys were taken from their mothers at the age of seven and lived in soldiers' barracks until the age of thirty. Spartans believed in rigid discipline, courage, and hardiness. They saw no purpose in pleasurable pursuits. Their way of life was what we would call, well, *spartan.*

If Spartans had had a motto, it might well have been Deeds, not words. Spartans were known for the terseness of their remarks. It is said that an enemy general was headed for Laconia, the region that had Sparta as its capital. The general threatened, "If I enter Laconia, I will level Sparta to the ground." The Spartans' reply was just one word: "If."

It is no surprise that people of few words are called *laconic.* President Calvin Coolidge came from New England, an American region noted for the spartan qualities of some of its inhabitants. According to one story, a dinner guest turned to Coolidge and said, "Mr. President, I have just made a bet that I can make you say more than two words to me."

The President replied laconically, "You lose."

Two hundred years before their war with Sparta, the people of Athens tasted harsh and rigid rule. A legislator named Draco drew up the laws of Athens for the first time. Draco's legal code was, to say the least, severe. The punishment for owing money was enslavement. Death was the more common punishment for other crimes. Today stern measures that are harsher than they need to be are described as *draconian*.

According to Greek mythology, the earliest gods were the huge and powerful Titans. The Titans were eventually overthrown by the gods of Mount Olympus, whose names are more familiar to readers of myths today. Titans who *are* familiar include the father of all the Titans, Uranus, whose name survived to serve, in 1781, as the label for the newly discovered seventh planet from the sun. The largest moon of the planet Saturn is called Titan. And the element names *uranium* and *titanium* come from the same sources.

The word *titan* can refer to any giant: a seven-foot-tall basketball-playing titan, or a business titan who wields great power. The adjective *titanic* describes someone or something of great size and strength. But because of the fate of the ship *Titanic* in 1912 (on its first voyage, it hit an iceberg and sank, and more than 1,500 passengers drowned), the word makes people think of a horrible disaster. That association is the reason the name *Titanic* is not likely to be applied to ships, buildings, bridges, or large desserts anytime soon.

We use the name of one Titan whenever we ask for a special kind of reference book. According to Greek myth, the Titan Atlas was punished by the god Zeus and forced to hold the heavens on his shoulders. In the sixteenth century, the geographer Gerhard Kremer, better known as Mercator, published a map collection. On the title page, he showed Atlas carrying the world on his back. Ever since that time, a book of maps has been called an *atlas*.

Monsters were common in ancient myths. Like the sea-nymph sirens, they were often part human and part animal. Echidna (ih-KID-nuh), for example, was half woman and half serpent. She was mother to a number of other monsters, including the Chimaera (ky-MEER-uh). The Chimaera was a female monster who breathed fire and looked something like a lion, goat, and serpent combined. Today the *echidna* is a small Australian mammal that eats insects. It is monstrous only in the sense that it is unusual. It is a monotreme, a mammal that lays eggs. The word *chimera* is used to label any strange and foolish flight of the imagination. Unrealistic hopes may be said to be *chimerical.*

The gods of Greek mythology often punished mortals for the sin of pride. Zeus had fathered a mortal named Tantalus and showed him special treatment. Tantalus was ungrateful. He learned of ambrosia—the secret food that could be eaten only by the gods. Tantalus tasted it. He even shared it with his friends. For this crime and for other wickedness (Tantalus served up pieces of his own son at a banquet), Zeus punished Tantalus. Tantalus underwent severe and eternal torture in Hades, the Greek land of the dead. He was forced to stand in the middle of a refreshing lake beneath branches filled with ripe, delicious fruit. But amidst this plenty, he suffered endless thirst and gnawing hunger. If Tantalus lowered his head to drink the water, the lake dried up immediately. If he lifted his arm to an overhanging branch, it pulled back out of reach. From the name *Tantalus* comes the English verb *to tantalize.* Have you ever been tantalized by something so tantalizing that you wanted it more than anything? Too bad.

Ancient Greeks believed in a nature god who watched over pastures, forests, and grazing animals. The god had the lower body of a goat and the upper body of a man, and was often depicted playing a seven-reed flute. The instrument is still played today and is known as a Pan pipe, for the god's name was Pan. Pan was not a lovely fellow to come upon in the woods. His appearances were sudden and startling. He inspired fear in his viewers, who usually ran off in all directions because they were *panic*-stricken.

If you feel panic, perhaps you have a *phobia*. According to the Greeks, the god of war had two sons, Phobos and Deimos; both names meant "fear." (Those names are today used for the twin moons of the planet Mars, which is named after the Roman god of war.)

Phobos' name shows up in the English word *phobia*, "an intense, unreasonable, and abnormal fear." It also shows up as a suffix added to all the names for things that human beings are abnormally afraid of. The list is long.

Victims of *claustrophobia* ("fear of closed places") feel more comfortable outdoors, where they are not likely to bump into anyone suffering from *agoraphobia* ("fear of open places"). Many people have *acrophobia* ("fear of high places"), while those with *bathophobia* ("fear of deep places") should probably choose careers other than mining. Miners and cave explorers are not likely to have *anginophobia* ("fear of narrow places") or *scotophobia* ("fear of darkness"). Barbers should not have *pogonophobia* ("fear of beards"), and it could be awkward if a dentist developed *odontophobia* ("fear of teeth"). The construction industries do not attract many victims of *gephyrophobia* ("fear of crossing a bridge") or *batophobia* ("fear of passing high buildings"). People with *tachophobia* ("fear of speed") don't need to be told not to race cars for a living. Regardless of what career choices people make, anyone can develop *ergophobia* ("fear of work"). That problem can be offset, however, by a touch of *peniaphobia* ("fear of poverty"), which is not likely to be accompanied by *chrometaphobia* ("fear of money").

Many of us tremble on hearing a good ghost story, and it's sensible to be afraid of robbers. These fears become overwhelming to the unfortunate people troubled by *phasmophobia* ("fear of ghosts") and *harpaxophobia* ("fear of robbers").

Who enjoys seeing a mouse scurrying across the kitchen floor? Not many people, and certainly not anyone with *musophobia* ("fear of mice"). Lots of people have *herpetophobia* ("fear of reptiles") or more specifically, *ophidiophobia* ("fear of snakes"). Alfred Hitchcock's famous 1963 chiller *The Birds* may well have inspired a few cases of *ornithophobia* ("fear of birds"). Crawly, creepy creatures are not usually looked on with affection; that general attitude may explain *vermiphobia* ("fear of worms") and *arachnephobia* ("fear of spiders"). People with *hippophobia* ("fear of horses") can usually avoid the problem, unlike victims of *zoophobia* ("fear of animals").

There are people with *astraphobia* ("fear of lightning"), *mysophobia* ("fear of dirt"), *gymnophobia* ("fear of nudity"), *cnidophobia* ("fear of insect stings"), and good ol' *triskaidekaphobia*

159

("fear of the number 13"). Those with *logophobia* ("fear of words") have probably not been able to reach this sentence. When phobias get out of control, victims may be said to have *panphobia* ("fear of everything"). And what do you think *phobophobia* is?

Even though the examples above all show *-phobia* attached to Greek word roots, why not take the liberty of adding the suffix to roots of your choice? Your listeners would immediately understand the meanings of such creations as *examophobia*, *homeworkophobia*, or *computerphobia*. Such new words illustrate one way in which words enter English—through the building up of known parts.

VI
New Words
and Changed Words

As you've seen in the last chapter, and in Chapter II, new words are commonly made by combining known parts. This chapter offers several more examples of words that have been stretched through such additions. You will also discover words that have been created and transformed by other methods. Stories of new words and changed words are a big part of a bigger story, of course—the story that tells why we use the words we do.

Stretched and Squeezed Words

In 1869, the English Parliament passed a controversial act. The act said that the Irish Episcopal Church would cease to exist after 1871. The Episcopal Church had been the state church of Ireland, and Irish citizens had been required to support it, even though almost all of them were Catholics. The 1869 law was called the Disestablishment Act, because

163

it **dis**established the authority of the Episcopal Church. Those who opposed this disestablishment were **anti**disestablishment and were therefore known as *antidisestablishmentarians.* Their position was called *antidisestablishmentarianism.* And that is the source of the wonderfully long word that schoolchildren have prided themselves on pronouncing and spelling for more than a century.

Antidisestablishmentarianism is a *sesquipedalian* (SES-kwih-puh-DAY-lee-un) word, "long and made of many parts." *Sesqui* in Latin means "one and a half," and *ped* means "foot," so a sesquipedalian word is a foot and a half long . . . at least it seems to stretch that length.

Perhaps the longest word in English is the name for a lung disease. The disease affects miners who breathe in dust particles as they break up rocks. The Greek combining form for "lung" is *pneumon.* Dust particles are extremely small, or *ultramicroscopic.* They are made from rocks, which contain the element *silicon* and may be formed from *volcanoes.* The Greek combining form for "dust" is *konis,* or *conis.* And the name for the disease? *pneumonoultramicroscopicsilicovolcanoconiosis.*

Few of such stretched words approach the 45-letter length of *pneumonoultramicroscopicsilicovolcanoconiosis.* But those that do may be names for chemical compounds. When chemical elements combine to form compounds, the word elements in their names combine too. A dangerous pesticide once in widespread use was *dichlorodiphenyltrichloroethane.* Rachel Carson (1907–64), a scientist and writer, exposed the environmental damage caused by this pesticide, and soon millions of people were demanding that it be banned. The pesticide name became well-known, but only in its short and pronounce-able form: DDT.

DDT is a shortened form called an abbreviation. Abbreviations are especially common in the fields of science and technology. Think of how unwieldy it would be to say or write *dichlorodiphenyltrichloroethane* every time you referred to DDT. Or to repeat *methyltrinitrobenzene* in a discussion of the explosive known familiarly as TNT. What about saying *deoxyribonucleic acid* with every mention of the genetic material known as DNA?

The English language has always had stretched words be-cause speakers have always made new words by combining parts of old ones. That natural tendency to stretch can lead to the opposite tendency—to squeeze. If a stretched word becomes too long, people use shortened, or clipped, forms instead. Abbreviations are just one solution. There are other squeezed forms too.

Quick! Call a *cab*! The vehicle name *cab* has been squeezed from a much longer term: *taximeter cabriolet*. Cabriolet (KAB-ree-oh-LAY) was the French name for a small horse-drawn two-wheeled carriage that leaped over bumps in the road (*cabriole* is related to *caper*, a word for the leaping motion of animals). In the 1800's, English speakers shortened the vehicle name to *cab*. The *taximeter* part referred to the tax rate, or fare, that passengers paid, and is the source of a synonym. Quick! Call a *taxi*!

Not everyone can afford to ride in taxis or cabs. A less

expensive mode of transportation is the *bus*. *Bus* is a word squeezed from *voiture omnibus*, "carriage for everyone."

Another vehicle is the jeep. Jeeps were originally created for the army during World War II. They were designed to be a tough, all-purpose form of transportation. The word *jeep* was made from the letters GP, the initials of the army's original name for the vehicle: general purpose.

On the same roadways traveled by taximeter cabriolets, voitures omnibus, and general-purpose vehicles, you can see *caravans* of all sizes. You would probably call the vehicles by their common, squeezed name, however: *vans*. The word *caravan* originally referred to a line of travelers crossing the desert.

Speaking of vehicles . . . here are two riddles.

1. Question: When is a dog especially good at pulling loads?
   Answer: When its tail is a-waggin'.

2. Question: Why is a poodle that is in an automobile falling off a cliff such a magical thing to see?
   Answer: Because it's a flying car-pet.

If those riddles made you groan, it's because of the painful *pun* in each. A pun is a form of word play that depends on different meanings for words that sound alike. Although English speakers and writers have always enjoyed making such punishing word plays, the word *pun* did not appear until the 1600's. It was squeezed from an Italian word that meant "fine point": *pundigrion*.

166

Here is another joke with a pun in the punchline. Can you guess what other word in the riddle has been squeezed from a longer word?

Arnie: I just tried to call the zoo, but I couldn't get through.
Ernie: Why not?
Arnie: The lion was busy.

If you guessed that *zoo* is a shortened word, you were right. The original term for the place was *zoological garden* or *zoological park* (the word *zoological* refers to the study of animal life).

One squeezed word has been around for four hundred years. Today it is spelled *good-by* or *goodbye* or *good-bye*. It used to be spelled *Godbwye*, which hints at the original, longer expression. Parting speakers used to say, "God be with you."

Another expression that has been shortened is *of the clock*. Speakers found that it took less time to say *o'clock* instead.

Hundreds of years ago, London's Hospital of St. Mary of Bethlehem was converted into an asylum for the insane. Since treatment of the mentally ill was unknown at that time, inmates were simply locked up together. The place was noisy, wild, and frightening. Referring to the asylum, speakers gradually squeezed the name *Bethlehem* into *Bedlam*, which has since been used to name any place or condition of noisy disorder.

Bedlam may be the result whenever a crowd gathers. Long ago, English writers used the Latin words *mobile vulgus* ("moving crowd") or just *mobile* (which they probably pronounced MOB-

167

ih-lee), to describe the common, or vulgar, folk. These lower classes, it was thought, were quickly moved—they were changeable and easy to arouse. The Latin term has since been shortened to a form that sounds not at all scholarly: *mob*.

Here is a paragraph with several squeezed words in it. Can you find them? (Answers are at the bottom of the page.)

Listen to Mendrick as he plays the piano! Just last week the flu had sapped him of all strength. Now he is keen to play soccer again, watch movies, and go to the gym with his pals.

One category of squeezed forms is the portmanteau word. *Portmanteau*, which comes from an Old French word meaning "coat carrier," is the name for a two-part suitcase. Lewis Carroll, the nineteenth-century writer, coined the term *portmanteau word* to describe two words that were squeezed together so that "there are two meanings packed up in one word." Carroll himself filled the nonsense poem "Jabberwocky" with many portmanteau words, some of which are now part of English vocabulary. The hero of the poem, for example, after slaying the Jabberwock, "went *galumphing* back." To describe the hero's peculiar pace, Carroll invented a portmanteau word, a combination of *gallop* and *triumph* —*galumph*.

(Answers: *Piano* was originally *pianoforte*, formed from the Italian words *piano*, "softly," and *forte*, "loudly." *Flu* comes from *influenza*, the Italian name for the disease, related to the word *influence*. *Soccer* comes from the British name *association football*. *Movies* were originally *moving pictures*. And *gym* comes from *gymnasium*, the Latin name for a school in which athletes trained naked.)

Another verse from "Jabberwocky":

> *"And hast thou slain the Jabberwock?*
> *Come to my arms, my beamish boy!*
> *O frabjous day! Callooh! Callay!"*
> *He chortled in his joy.*

The portmanteau word *chortle*, made from *snort* and *chuckle*, has made its way from "Jabberwocky" into speech, writing, and dictionaries.

The portmanteau word formed from *smoke* and *fog* is well-known to city dwellers who have suffered from the burning eyes and irritated lungs caused by *smog*.

Lazy Sundays are a good time to eat a late *breakfast*. Or is it an early *lunch*? A portmanteau word was needed to answer that question. It appeared about 1900: *brunch*.

Also at the turn of the twentieth century, an American humorist invented a portmanteau word that was quickly adopted by English speakers. The word described the short paragraphs of high praise found on book jackets, enticing readers to buy the book. The word was formed by squeezing together *blurt* ("a sudden statement") and *burble* ("a bubbling sound, as of running water"). Have you read any good *blurbs* lately?

There is no doubt that the automobile changed Americans' lives and vocabulary. As motorists began to drive long distances on brand-new highways, they needed places to stay. The *motor hotels* that sprang up to serve them were soon called *motels*.

In the early twentieth century, a chemist created a substance used for wrapping. It was a thin transparent material made from wood pulp, or cellulose. The chemist created a name for the material by combining the word *cellulose* with the Greek word for "transparent," *phanein*. The resulting portmanteau word is now well-known: *cellophane*. *Cellophane* was originally spelled with a capital letter because it was a trademark. A trademark is a name that a manufacturer protects by law. Sometimes these trademarks, or brand names, are used so often that they become common nouns, despite the manufacturer's efforts to stop people from using the trademark as a general term. That is how the trademark *Cellophane* became the common noun *cellophane*. Trademarks are one source of new words, and the subject of the next section.

Invented Words

When new products are invented, their names must be invented too. Today some language experts specialize in coming up with business and product names that will sound memorable and appealing to consumers. In the days before such specialization, manufacturers and inventors created their own names for new items. But in both the past and the present, product namers have relied on two standard methods: They put together known word parts in new ways, or they use pleasant-sounding syllables to create brand-new brand names.

Like the creator of Cellophane (discussed in the last section), some inventors devised trademarks by combining existing word parts. And like *cellophane*, some of those trademarks have made themselves so comfortable in English that they have lost their protected status and are spelled with a lowercase letter. The word *mimeograph*, for example, entered English with a capital *M*, as the trademark for a then-new page-duplicating process. (Today photocopy machines do most duplicating of pages, along with Ditto duplicators, which are still found in schools—note the capital *D* signifying *Ditto* as a protected trademark. But for years mimeograph machines were the main source of copies, or "mimeos.") The name *Mimeograph* was made by putting together part of a Greek word that means "to imitate" and the combining form *-graph-*, which refers to anything written or drawn. Similarly, a British inventor patented a new optical instrument in 1817. He used a Greek word meaning "beautiful form" along with the combining form *-scope-*, which refers to sight, to create *Kaleidoscope*, which lost its capital *K* long ago.

In 1863, a patent was granted for a new floor covering that used linseed (sometimes called flaxseed) oil as one of its components. The manufacturer created a name for the product by combining the Latin words for "flax" and "oil," *linum* and *oleum*. Linoleum Floor Cloth has been underfoot for so long that we now simply call it *linoleum*.

In 1900, the moving stairway was introduced by the Otis Elevator Company. Its name was a trademark: *Escalator*. The name was based on the word *escalade*, "to scale, or climb, a wall." The reason the invention was not simply called an Escalader was that the suffix *-ator* appeared in the name of

Otis's other, already successful creation, the *elevator*. Over time and through much use, the trademark has become the common noun *escalator*.

Another well-known item also made its first appearance just before the start of the twentieth century. The German manufacturers of this miracle drug combined elements of its chemical name (in English, *acetylsalicylic acid*) to create a trademark: *Aspirin*. Because aspirin has been the pill to swallow for about a century, the word is now spelled with a small *a*.

In 1925, the B. F. Goodrich Company invented a rubber-coated boot with an easy-to-use fastener on it. The company created a name for the boot by combining *zip*, an existing word suggesting speed and energy, with the suffix *-er*. The trademark was registered as *Zipper*. The word *zipper* is now, of course, a common noun applied to fastening devices found on many more items than boots. What was the original term for the device? The now-lost *slide fastener*.

In addition to adapting known words or word parts to create names for new products, manufacturers have occasionally relied on sound more than on meaning. The originators of a toy made from a spool and a string came up with a trademark that suggested both childlike speech and continuous motion: *Yo-yo*. That name has worked so well, in fact, that the toy cannot be described by any other label. The capital *Y*, signifying a protected trademark, disappeared long ago.

Among the synthetic fibers that have been created in the chemistry laboratories of textile companies is nylon. *Nylon* was not registered as a trademark, but it was coined by its manufacturer, the DuPont company. Like *yo-yo*, the word was created purely by sound—its parts have no meaning. As new synthetic fibers followed the creation of nylon, they were given trademarks with similar-sounding names: *Dacron* and *Orlon*.

When manufacturers go to the trouble of creating product names and registering them as trademarks, they fight the loss of those trademarks. They do not like to see their brand names appear in print as common nouns. Eventually, however, the legal costs of protecting a trademark become too great, and the name appears ever more frequently without its capital letter. Some words, such as *yo-yo* and *escalator*, have already entered dictionaries as common nouns. Other trademarks that are still protected, however, are used freely as general terms in everyday speech. Consider the list below. Every item is a general term for which the still-protected trademark is in common use. Can you tell what trademark matches each?

1. gelatin dessert
2. petroleum jelly
3. cellophane tape
4. cotton swabs
5. table tennis
6. photocopying process
7. nonstick coating (chemical name *polytetrafluorethylene*)
8. lip balm
9. plastic wrap
10. adhesive bandages
11. plastic foam or polystyrene plastic
12. self-adhesive plastic paper
13. nylon fastening tape
14. facial tissues
15. elasticized bandage

Here are the brand-name answers: 1. Jell-O®. 2. Vaseline®. 3. Scotch® tape. 4. Q-tips®. 5. Ping-Pong®. 6. Xerox®. 7. Teflon®. 8. Chapstick®. 9. Saran® wrap. 10. Band-Aids®. 11. Styrofoam®. 12. Con-Tact® paper. 13. Velcro®. 14. Kleenex®. 15. Ace® bandage.

Some of those names are sure to enter dictionaries as common nouns and adjectives — it is only a matter of time.

A trademark is just one kind of invented word. What makes trademarks unusual is that their origins can be reliably traced. Because a name used as a trademark must be legally registered, we can tell when the word was born and who its parents were. It is not common to find such recorded birth dates for other words. Still, we do know when Lewis Carroll penned his portmanteau inventions *galumph* and *chortle* (mentioned in the previous section); and we also know when certain other invented words made their first appearance in print.

The great English poet John Milton published the epic poem *Paradise Lost* in 1667. In it was a word he invented as a name for the capital of Hell, ruled by Satan and populated by demons. He called the place *Pandemonium*. As with most invented words, *pandemonium* was based on earlier roots — in this case on Greek word parts meaning "all demons." Today the word *pandemonium* refers to any state of wild disorder or chaos.

Speaking of chaos, the Greek word *chaos* was the name for empty space, and the source of another invented word. Jan Baptista van Helmont (1577–1644) was a Belgian chemist who needed a name for the formless matter present everywhere. He took *chaos*, made a few sound changes, and invented the word *gas*. Helmont also invented another word: *blas*. It described the influence of the stars on weather, and it went the way of many coinages — it never came into general use.

The American sculptor Alexander Calder (1898–1977) is credited with creating a form of sculpture made of parts that move in the breeze. He invented a name for his creations by borrowing a form of the Latin word for "move." He called his sculptures *mobiles.* The word *mobile* (MOH-beel) quickly entered English as the name for any sculpture that hangs, spins, or flutters.

As with trademarks, some invented words convey their meaning through their sounds. A popular British comedian named Arthur Roberts (1852–1933) created a silly card game in which players tried to fool one another. He gave the game a nonsensical name: *spoof.* The word *spoof* has since been used to refer to a practical joke and to a mild kind of satire or parody.

The American mathematician Edward Kasner (1878–1955) was accustomed to working with numbers expressed in scientific notation. In the system of scientific notation, 10^{10} (ten to the tenth power) is the numeral 1 followed by ten zeros; in American English that number is called ten billion. Kasner decided to create a name for the number 10^{100} (ten to the one hundredth power), or 1 followed by 100 zeros. It was his young nephew who came up with a word for such an unimaginably enormous quantity. If you have 1000 000000000000000000000000000000000000000000000 00000000000000000000000000000000000000000000 of something, you have a *googol.* The word *googol* is now sometimes used as the name for any huge, huge number.

Maury Maverick was a U.S. congressman from Texas in

the 1930's. He came up with a funny-sounding word to describe the hard-to-understand language of government bureaucrats. Maverick preferred plain and clear talk to the sesquipedalian words and circuitous sentences he was hearing so much of in the capital. He was fed up with what he called (and what we still call) *gobbledygook.*

Language historians do not agree that Maury Maverick was the *very* first person to say the word *gobbledygook,* even though it is clearly an invented word, and he is usually credited with its invention. Sometimes it is difficult to pinpoint the precise origin of an invented word. Even the inventor may be unaware that a word is being formed. It was another U.S. congressman who became the unwitting source of such a new word.

In 1817, the voters of Buncombe County, North Carolina, elected Felix Walker as their representative to Congress. Congressman Walker became notorious for longwinded speeches that never seemed to come to the point. Bored listeners often got up and left when one of Walker's speeches began. But the congressman from Buncombe County was not bothered. The purpose of his speeches was to impress the voters back home. "I am not speaking for your ears," he once told the departing crowd. "I am only talking for Buncombe." The line became famous, and soon any speech that was filled with more foolishness than sense was said to be "for Buncombe." Not long afterward, such empty talk, known as *bunkum,* received the shortened label still used today: *bunk.*

The source of one word has been the subject of much

research and debate. The origin of this word has aroused great interest because the word is used countless times daily by speakers of American English. It is a word that has a peculiarly American sound but has also spread all over the world. It may well be the first English word learned by almost all speakers of other languages. What is the word? Okay, okay, you've had enough of an introduction, here's the word: *okay* (also spelled *O.K.* or *OK*).

The most carefully researched explanation to date points to more than one source. The complicated story begins with events in Boston, Massachusetts, in 1838. Journalists and editors of the time were peppering their news articles with abbreviations, just for fun. They wrote *n.g.*, for example, to stand for the phrase *no go*. More language playfulness was shown soon after, when the same expression was abbreviated *k.g.*, standing for the purposely misspelled version *know go*. Writers also used *a.r.* to stand for *all right*, and *o.w.* to stand for the humorously misspelled variation *oll wright*.

People were already using these and other initials in their speech. They may have been saying *O.K.*, too, before the letters made their first recorded appearance in print in 1839. The letters *O.K.* stood for a term of approval, *all correct*, as if misspelled *oll korrect*.

This fad of using initials spread to other cities. The abbreviation *O.K.* meaning "all correct" was beginning to travel to speakers and writers beyond Boston. But another event was taking place in 1840. And that event—a heated presidential campaign—was to make *O.K.* widely popular.

In 1840, the Democrats were eager to see their candidate, Martin Van Buren, elected to a second term. In New York, Van Buren's home state, many political clubs sprang up to support him. One of those clubs was called the Democratic O.K. Club. Its members kept the meaning of *O.K.* secret, in order to arouse curiosity and lend an air of mystery to their proceedings. The letters actually stood for *Old Kinderhook,* a popular nickname for Van Buren, who had grown up in Kinderhook, New York.

The Democrats' opponents, the Whigs, made fun of the letters *O.K.* In newspaper editorials, they suggested some outrageous meanings for these secret letters. They said, for example, that the retired president and Democratic leader Andrew Jackson was the original writer of the letters *O.K.* They claimed that Jackson, being ill educated, thought that *O.K.* stood for *Ole Kurrek* or *Ole Korrect,* which they said was Jackson's ignorant way of spelling *all correct.* Or they claimed that the letters *O.K.* were really meant to be read backwards, and stood for *kicked out.* They also said that *O.K.* meant "Out of Kash" or "Out of Karacter." As a result of all these appearances in newsprint—and on the banners paraded by members of the Democratic O.K. Club—the abbreviation *O.K.* was getting a lot of attention. In a matter of months, the letters *O.K.,* as a positive term ("all correct"), were being heard and seen everywhere.

Even though supporters rallied to the cause of O.K. (Old Kinderhook), Van Buren lost the election. But the expression of approval, *O.K.,* had become part of American English.

Restless Words

What are *restless* words? Words that don't stand still. Words that find new meanings or new popularity as new generations of speakers use them, words that shed old meanings or disappear entirely, words that revive after years of silence, words that take on narrower meanings, words that take on broader meanings, words that change, change, change.

Open to any page of a good dictionary, and see how many entries have numbered definitions after them. A word can mean one thing or something slightly different or something else completely. And if you skim any English literary work of a past age (a play by Shakespeare, for example), you'll find many examples of what dictionaries label Archaic or Obsolete—words no longer spoken or printed. You'll also find words that no longer appear in dictionaries at all.

If the chapters in this book have made their point at all, it is that language is a living thing. Change is part of any life. In a sense, all words are restless. But some words have fidgeted in an especially fascinating way.

It might surprise you to know that *girls* once meant "boys," and *boys* once meant "slaves." In Middle English, the word *girle* or *gurle* referred to a child of either sex. The Middle English *boye* or *baye* referred to a male servant before it began to be used for any male child. The word *boy* may be derived from a Latin word for "fetters," the chains of bondage. (To confuse matters further, by Shakespeare's time, a boy was a *boy* and a girl was a *child*.)

If you were trying to sell a product, would you describe it as *cheap* and *crummy*? That depends on whether you want customers. But the *crumb* used to be the best part of a loaf of bread—the part that wasn't the crust. And when Americans first began to use the adjective *crumby* or *crummy*, they meant it as high praise. Then a slang use of *crumb* and *crumby* (or *crummy*) to mean "louse" and "lousy" began to appear. If you think about the tickling, crawly sensation caused by a crumb that has fallen on your skin, you may see the connection between *crumb* and *louse*. The positive meaning for *crumby* was eventually replaced by the negative one.

The word *cheap* comes from an Old English word for "barter." By Shakespeare's time, *cheapen* meant "to sell." A buyer who found a "good cheap" was quite pleased with the quality and price of the purchased product. An inexpensive product is not always of good quality, however. It may be poorly made. So it was that *cheap* came to mean "shoddy." *Cheap* and *crummy* have certainly changed for the worse over time.

If your friends told you that a movie was "just awful," would you rush to get in line for a ticket? Probably not. But *awful* was made from *awe* and *ful*, and something *awful* used to fill one with awe. Today we use the word *awesome* to describe a positive experience and reserve *awful* for the negative. English speakers are doing something similar with words that are derived from the Latin word *terrere*, "to frighten." Think of how you use the words *terrible* and *terrifying*. Both words can mean "dreadful and frightening." But there

180

is a third word that has changed into a description for something positive, something magnificent, something that's, well, *terrific!*

People used to believe that the human body was regulated by four *humors.* The word *humor* comes from a Latin word for "fluid or liquid" (you can see the same root in the modern English word *humid*), and the four principal humors were blood, phlegm, yellow bile, and black bile. Medieval medicine was based on understanding the relationships among the humors; it was thought that humors determined a person's mood or character. Someone with a rich supply of blood, for example, was *sanguine* (from the Latin word for "blood"), or energetic and cheerful. Someone with phlegm as the dominant humor was *phlegmatic,* or calm and unexcitable; someone with too much yellow bile (choler) was *choleric,* or angry; and black bile caused *melancholy,* or sadness. We still speak of being in an "ill or bad humor," but today the word *humor* (along with *humorous* and *humorist*) makes us think of wit, fun, and laughter. It is not clear how the change happened. Perhaps it began with two immensely popular comedies by the English poet and dramatist Ben Jonson (1573–1637). In *Every Man in His Humour* (which, by the way, had an actor in the cast named William Shakespeare) and its sequel *Every Man Out of His Humour,* Jonson created comic characters. Each was dominated by one quality, or humor. These characters, with names like Wellbred, Downright, and Brainworm, made audiences laugh uproariously. Perhaps the word *humor* was becoming associated with amusement as a result. Yet it took about two more centuries before a *sense of humor* was seen as a trait worth smiling about. And a *humorist* is now someone who writes amusing stories and is not (as described in 1755 in an early English dictionary) "one who has violent and peculiar passions."

Would your listeners understand what you meant if you described someone or something as "pretty nice"? They probably would sense that you had positive feelings of some sort, but those two words are notoriously imprecise. Those words have been so restless over the centuries that their meanings are no longer sharp.

Back in Anglo-Saxon times, *pretty* was used to mean "tricky or deceitful." Gradually a related but more positive meaning emerged—something *pretty* was "clever." The word was also used, as it still is, ironically or disdainfully (That's a *pretty* matter, isn't it!) *Pretty* also meant "elegant" (What a *pretty* gown!) or "large" (What a *pretty* pile of coins!) Today something *pretty* is pleasantly attractive, though not quite beautiful. And the word is frequently used as an adverb to mean "somewhat": *pretty good*, *pretty bad*, *pretty near*, *pretty far*, and even *pretty ugly*.

Few words have undergone as many meaning changes as *nice*. Middle English speakers used *nice* to describe someone foolish and ignorant. After a century of use, the word was describing people (usually women) who were shyly coy; and later, women who were not at all shy (in other words, not "nice" at all). Then that meaning, "wanton," was accompanied by an entirely different one—"particular and fastidious," which is a meaning that has been passed down to modern speakers. We can still mention a *nice bit of handiwork* ("skillfully done") or a *nice distinction* ("fine and subtle"). But American speakers decided to use the word vaguely—and often—as a general term of approval. Nice job! Nice shoes! Nice haircut! Nice party! Nice kid! And in the overused expression "Have a nice day!"

Among the vague words we use nonstop is a noun that can name, well, anything. Suppose you can't remember what something is called. Just point, and have a conversation like this one:

> "Please pass me the . . . the . . . thing."
> "What thing?"
> "That thing, over there."
> "Oh, you mean this thing?"
> "No, the thing with the thing on it."
> "This thing, or that thing?"
> "Yes, that's the thing. Thanks."
> "It was nothing."

If you look up *thing* in the dictionary, you'll see what a difficult time dictionary writers have had trying to define a word that can mean anything. It was much easier back in the days of Old English, when *thing* started out with a specific meaning. It was the name for a gathering of lawmakers. Gradually the word took on more and more meanings—

not just "a meeting" but the "deeds or acts" that resulted from the meeting, then any "matter" at all.

Thing began with a specific meaning and over time acquired a more general one. Other nouns have begun as general names and have narrowed in meaning over time. Take *meat*, for example.

Meat used to refer to any solid food, not just food from an animal. Old English speakers called food from an animal "flesh-meat," breads and cakes "bake-meat," and food chopped into fine pieces "mince-meat." (*Mincemeat* is still the name for the chopped mixture that fills mince pie.) Our modern menus offer far more specialized items than the simple "meat and drink" of old.

Sometimes as words change in meaning, remnants of their old meanings are left behind. Did you ever wonder why soldiers or campers eat at a *mess* hall, for example? Are they supposed to make a mess? Or clean it up? Actually, a *mess* was once "a portion of food" placed on a dish. That meaning, which was in use for centuries, has been replaced by the modern meaning—suggested by what a lumpish mound of food sometimes looks like when it's dolloped onto a plate.

Have you ever seen those gurgling bogs of quicksand depicted in the movies? The hapless victim takes one false step . . . and down, down he goes, screaming all the way until he disappears, swallowed by the swamp. Does *quick*sand really act that *quick*ly? No, the *quick* in the name has nothing to do with speed; it reveals an original-but-lost word meaning. The word *quick* used to mean "alive," and the rolling, sucking motion of quicksand does indeed make it seem like a living thing. In Middle English, *quick* also meant "swift" and "lively," and those are the familiar meanings that have been handed down. Except for the meaning buried in *quicksand*, of course.

Have you ever read about a brave and *plucky* lad who had plenty of *pluck*? Even though *pluck* and *plucky* are less common than they were just a generation or two ago, the words are still used today to describe bold and resourceful behavior. What does boldness have to do with plucking? When we use the word *pluck*, we are usually describing something we do to stringed instruments, flowers, eyebrows, or chickens—a pulling, tugging, grasping motion. But precisely because of that motion, *pluck* once had another meaning. Pluck was what a cook plucked out of the chest of a slaughtered animal: the heart, liver, and lungs. From *pluck* as a word for "innards" to *pluck* as a word for "spirited courage" is not as great a leap in meaning as it first may seem. After all, think of the words we use today instead of *pluck* and *plucky*: What *guts*! The guy sure is *gutsy*!

MY DREAM

Here is a dream.
It is my dream.
My own dream.
I dreamt it.
I dreamt that my hair was kempt.
Then I dreamt that my true love unkempt it.

OGDEN NASH

The poet Ogden Nash was a master of word play. What makes his little verse above amusing is the sheer silliness of the word *unkempt*. *Unkempt* is in every dictionary (it means "uncombed" or "untidy"), but *kempt* is not. If something can be unkempt, why can't it be kempt? Well, once it could. The word *kempt* did exist long ago (in Middle English, the word *kemben* meant "to comb"), but it disappeared. We have only its opposite, *unkempt*, to play with.

He: Did you hear about John's friend Ruth?
She: No, what happened?
He: She fell out of the car he was driving.
She: How terrible! What did John do?
He: Nothing. He just drove on *ruthlessly*.

Ruthless ("cruel and merciless") is another word that seems to be missing a counterpart. Was there ever a word *ruth*? Yes, there was, but it is no longer used in ordinary language. As you can probably guess, *ruth* meant "compassion" or "pity."

A ruthless driver, like John above, may also be called reckless. Here again, only the suffixed word, *reckless*, has survived. It used to be possible to say, "This reckless person does not reck the danger." But *reck* is gone, replaced by synonyms such as *heed*, *mind*, or *pay attention to*.

You can be *overwhelmed* by just about anything that brings out a strong emotional response. Terror, beauty, love, friendship, excitement—all can seem to "wash over and engulf," which is the meaning of *overwhelm*. Well, if something can be overwhelming, can it be *whelming*? And just what does *whelm* mean? *Whelm* is in fact a modern English word, but it is not often heard or seen. Since *whelm* means "to wash over and engulf," it has been submerged by the word that means exactly the same thing: *overwhelm*.

Anyone who tries to use the word *couth* risks being called *uncouth*. The word *uncouth* (meaning "rude, ill-mannered, and not refined") is an English word, but *couth* was lost long ago. If you decide to describe a polite and refined person as very *couth*, do so with a wink. *Couth/uncouth* is another example of a word pair in which only one partner has survived. Long ago, *couth* meant "known" and "familiar" (we still have a remnant of that meaning in our expression *kith and kin,* meaning "friends and family"); *uncouth*, logically enough, meant "unknown" and "unfamiliar." But when *uncouth* began to move on to another meaning, referring to the ill-mannered behavior of strangers, the word *couth* was left behind.

Following the same pattern, the partnership of *ruly* and *unruly* split apart in the past. Today we speak of a disorderly classroom as *unruly*. But the place will not become *ruly*, even if ruled by a teacher with a ruler.

Pease porridge hot,
Pease porridge cold,
Pease porridge in the pot
Nine days old!
Nursery Rhyme

If you are familiar with that old rhyme, perhaps you've wondered what pease porridge was. Porridge, as anyone who has ever read about Goldilocks knows, is the hot breakfast cereal left behind by the Three Bears. But porridge used to be a thick soup. And pease porridge was a thick soup made from pease. But what were pease? Or more accurately, what *was* pease? *Pease* was the original name for a common vegetable; the singular form was *pease* (what you asked for when you wanted just one), and the plural form (used to refer to more than one) was *pesen.* The word *pease* was changed by English speakers who felt the need for a different singular form: *pea.* Now we can have one pea or many peas, but pease and pesen are things of the past.

Among other words that have changed their forms over the years are several that used to begin with vowels. English speakers have a natural tendency to rush the article *an* into the beginning vowel sound of the following noun. You may have heard young children say *a napple* instead of *an apple,* for example. Or *a negg* instead of *an egg.* Sometimes such forms become so widespread that they replace the earlier versions.

Speakers used to make fun of a trusting, or "innocent," person with the name *inny. What an inny!* became *What a ninny!*

Among English speakers, the practice of passing down a family name began about five hundred years ago. People used to have just one given name. As the population grew, additional names were used to distinguish people with the

188

same name. Three Harolds in a community, for example, might have been called Harold, the Small; Harold, of Woods; and Harold, the Smith. These "also names" were called *eke-names*. (*Eke* used to mean "also.") Through use, *an eke-name* became *a nickname.*

From a word related to *eft*, which is still the name for a small North American amphibian, English speakers called certain salamanders *ewts*. *An ewt* became *a newt*, which is the name we use today.

Occasionally speakers shifted the *n* sound away from the beginning of the word—and changed *a* to *an*. An unbiased person called in to settle a dispute was once *a noumper* (from the Old French words *non per*, "not equal"). Today *a noumper* is *an umpire.*

From an Old French word that meant "little cloth" came the Middle English word *naprun*. *A naprun* is now *an apron.*

The Arabic word *naranj*, the name for a citrus fruit, entered Middle English with its first *n* already gone. The *n* had been dropped by French speakers before they passed the name into English. That is why we know the fruit as *an orange.*

Movable sounds. Changeable meanings. Words are not fixed forever. Even as you read this, an imaginative writer or speaker may be changing an old word into a new one. And who can tell? Perhaps the new word will be appreciated and repeated. Soon another definition will begin to make its way into the dictionary.

A Few Final Words

The English language has more words than any other language on earth. One reason is that English has always borrowed words, not only from influential contributors like French and Latin, but also from languages as diverse as Algonquian, Malay, and Hebrew. English has borrowed from itself, too, re-creating new words from old parts. Our vocabulary is filled with compounds that name everything from *headhunters* to *toenails*; with affixed inventions that are *unmistakably*[1] *sesquipedalian*[2]; and with short words clipped from longer ones, so that we can be as brief as an *ad*[3], a *memo*[4], or a *recap*[5].

Wherever there are new ideas, there are needs for new names, which is why we have adopted invented words like

---

[1] *unmistakably*: un- + mis- + take + -able + -ly

[2] sesquipedalian (SES-kwih-puh-DAY-lee-un): long and made of many parts; said of words. From Latin *sesqui-*, "one and a half," and *ped*, "foot," a foot and a half in length.

[3] *ad*: shortened from *advertisement*

[4] *memo*: shortened from *memorandum*

[5] *recap*: shortened from *recapitulation*

yo-yo and eponymous ones like *sandwich*. Because a word is never limited to its original meaning, we can expand its uses with figurative meanings, as in this bit of advice: "Your grades may *yo-yo* if you *sandwich* all your studying between parties."

What does a word sound like when you say it? What are the different ways you use it? Why? The answers to these questions have to do with the ancient roots from which English words have grown and with the new routes those words have taken. You have seen some of those answers in the chapters of this book. You can discover more answers yourself, if you watch and listen . . . and open a dictionary.

Suggestions for Additional Reading

These books tell about the history and nature of the English language:

Is That Mother in the Bottle? Where Language Comes From and Where It Is Going by Jessica Davidson. New York: Franklin Watts, Inc., 1972.

The Tree of Language by Helene and Charlton Laird. Cleveland and New York: The World Publishing Company, 1957.

What a Funny Thing to Say! by Bernice Kohn. New York: The Dial Press, Inc., 1974.

These books tell about the origins of words and expressions:

Heavens to Betsy! and Other Curious Sayings. New York: Harper & Row, Publishers, 1986.

A Hog on Ice and Other Curious Expressions. New York: Harper & Row, Publishers, 1985.

Horsefeathers and Other Curious Words. New York: Harper & Row, Publishers, 1986.

Thereby Hangs a Tale: Stories of Curious Word Origins. New York: Harper & Row, Publishers, 1985.

The four titles above were originally published more than thirty years ago and were written by Charles Earle Funk, former editor-in-chief of the Funk & Wagnalls Standard Dictionary Series.

Wonders in Words by Maxwell Nurnberg. Englewood Cliffs, NJ: Prentice-Hall, Inc., 1968.

Wordly Wise by James McDonald. New York: Franklin Watts, Inc., 1984.

Word Mysteries and Histories: From Quiche to Humble Pie by the American Heritage Dictionary Editors. Boston: Houghton Mifflin Company, 1986.

Words: A Book About the Origins of Everyday Words and Phrases by Jane Sarnoff and Reynold Ruffins. New York: Charles Scribner's Sons, 1981.

These books tell about words that come from people's names:

Batty, Bloomers and Boycott: A Little Etymology of Eponymous Words by Rosie
    Boycott. New York: Peter Bedrick Books, 1983.
Word People by Nancy Caldwell Sorel. New York: American Heritage
    Publishing Company, 1970.

These books tell about English history:

Green Blades Rising: The Anglo-Saxons by Kevin Crossley-Holland. New
    York: The Seabury Press, Inc., 1976.
William the Conqueror and the Normans by Robin May. New York: Book-
    wright Press, 1985.

These are dictionaries that are available in most libraries:

American Heritage Dictionary. Boston: Houghton Mifflin Company.
Random House Dictionary of the English Language, 2nd unabridged edition.
    New York: Random House, Inc.
Webster's Compact Dictionary. Springfield, MA: Merriam-Webster.
Webster's New World Dictionary. New York: Simon & Schuster.
Webster's Third New International Dictionary of the English Language, Unabridged:
    The Great Library of the English Language. Springfield, MA: Merriam-
    Webster.
Webster's II New Riverside Dictionary. Boston: Houghton Mifflin Company.

The *Oxford English Dictionary*, published by Oxford University Press, is
a classic work and the most complete dictionary of the English language.
The second edition was published in 1989; its entries fill twenty volumes.
The OED, as it is called, is also available in a two-volume set.

Index

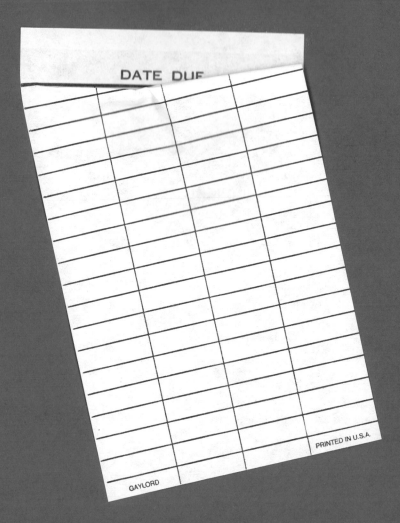

DATE DUE